Justice and Popular Culture

Justice and Popular Culture

Star Trek as Philosophical Text

George A. Gonzalez

LEXINGTON BOOKS
Lanham • Boulder • New York • London

Published by Lexington Books
An imprint of The Rowman & Littlefield Publishing Group, Inc.
4501 Forbes Boulevard, Suite 200, Lanham, Maryland 20706
www.rowman.com

6 Tinworth Street, London SE11 5AL

British Library Cataloguing in Publication Information Available

Library of Congress Cataloging-in-Publication Data Available

ISBN 978-1-7936-0241-1 (cloth : alk. paper)
ISBN 978-1-7936-0242-8 (electronic)

∞™ The paper used in this publication meets the minimum requirements of American National Standard for Information Sciences Permanence of Paper for Printed Library Materials, ANSI/NISO Z39.48-1992.

Contents

Introduction

The world system is in sharp crisis: global warming, the American (racist) Trump presidency, tensions between the United States and Russia, China (all nuclear powers), worldwide loss of biodiversity (deforestation, etc.), politically salient alt-right (white supremacist) elements, and political parties. A key reason that the world faces such immanent crises is because justice has been abandoned by modernity.[1] Democracy was the code for justice and it was the notion that countered another code for justice: communism. With the rise of neoliberalism (the free movement of capital, goods, and services worldwide), democracy has been stripped of its normative core and been reduced to procedures (elections, legal rules).[2] Democracy literally means rule by the people—more significantly, that sovereignty lies with the public (as opposed to a monarch, or aristocracy). It also implied that government, the state served the people (the public good).[3] Under the global neoliberalist regime, the state serves finance capital[4]—as communities, governments are reduced to attracting, maintaining investment by appeasing investors.[5] Public health, education, environmental protection, etc., are transactional as a result.[6]

In a context where the capital accumulation process and investor rights are the state's top priority, political power is increasingly vested in a clutch of political figures.[7] This is most prominently the case with the U.S. president—who today is more an elected dictator than a public official. Political scientists for many decades after World War Two wrote about the imperial presidency—where the Congress ceded more and more policymaking authority to the White House. With the presidency of George W. Bush (2001–2009) a qualitative political, legal shift occurred—the doctrine of the Unitary Executive. The Unitary Executive is a theory of presidential dictatorship—the federal government belongs to the occupant of the White House. Congress and the courts are purely advisory to the president.[8] The Bush administration illegally invaded and conquered Iraq; instituted programs of torture (enhanced interrogation) and indefinite detention without trial (Enemy Combatants); as well as mass spying (in direct contravention of the Constitution and the law).[9] The (opposition) Democratic Party acquiesced to this power grab by refusing to initiate impeachment proceedings after it gained a majority in both chambers of Congress in 2006. This pronounced concentration of political authority took place under the guise of the "Global War on Terror"—where the government publicly cast its top priority as the protection from ultra-stealthy, hyper-dangerous (foreign) radical elements.[10]

This political milieu aided the rise of Donald Trump and his subsequent installation as president in 2017. Trump's presidential campaign amplified and made sharply explicit the xenophobia of the War on Terror.[11] The Trump White House instituted a ban of virtually all visitors from seven countries (mostly Arab, Muslim nations)—speciously suggesting that there is something fundamentally flawed with these peoples.[12] Similarly, President Trump declared a national emergency to unilaterally allocate funds to build a "wall" to keep out immigrants from Mexico.[13] In Europe far right political parties are gaining salience and making a distinctive mark—promoting xenophobia.[14]

Under the auspices of "Make America Great Again,"[15] President Trump initiated a trade war with China,[16] and the United States is in open geopolitical competition with it.[17] The Democrats for their part are pushing the Trump administration to pursue a harder line against the Russian Putin government—politically sponsoring an investigation into the Russian government's putative involvement in the 2016 presidential campaign.[18]

The political deterioration of the world system,[19] overseen by the American government,[20] is accompanied by an acceleration of global ecological disaster—most clearly evident with the worsening catastrophe of global warming. Additionally, ecosystems around the world are being systematically destroyed and species numbers are correspondingly collapsing. Governments mostly stand idle in the face of what is the unfolding *sixth great extinction*—where upward of 90 percent of all life on Earth disappears.[21]

At the virtual dawn of industrial capitalism, Karl Marx foresaw the race to the bottom initiated by the increasing, ongoing automation of production. The greater and greater costs of building technologically advanced industry meant finance capital would over time demand cheaper and cheaper production factors, platforms to maximize investment returns (thereby distributing wealth upward).[22] Marx reasoned that this made capitalism inherently economically and politically unstable—cycling through one political, economic crisis after another, as wealth became more and more concentrated.[23] With global neoliberalism,[24] wealth has become especially concentrated (the Billionaire Class[25]) and crises afflict the entirety of the world's economy (e.g., the Great Recession of 2008).[26]

V. I. Lenin, building on Marx's argumentation, held international relations in the capitalist world system are inherently fluid—global (economic) power by necessity shifts from one country, region of the world to another. Such chronic imbalances create an unstable and violent global political milieu—dominant powers feel threatened as finance capital finds new (lower cost, higher profit) investment outlets.[27] Thus, China's becoming the new global center of (low wage) industrial investment[28] is viewed as a threat to U.S. global hegemonic authority.[29] In the effort to sustain the stability (profitability) of global capitalism, and countries seeking to maintain (increase) their political status in a competitive (dangerous) geopolitical landscape, the environment is recklessly sacrificed.[30]

As I noted above, the fundamental problem facing humanity is the absence of a coherent, universal conception of justice. Elite machinations are driven by the global quest for profit and power. At the same time, the environment is systematically destroyed, the possibility of nuclear war increases, and public health, education, etc., are deprioritized. Where is the justice in any of this? As already explained, democracy has been reduced to procedural rights (voting, fair trials)—procedures that can be readily corrupted[31] in a context where wealth is extremely concentrated[32] and the political elite are actively seeking to cow the population by continuously invoking menacing threats to public safety (for example, terrorism).[33] We need to return to the concept of communism if the world, society, and civilization are to be saved. Communism (as a notion of justice) has the virtue of being focused on outcome, not procedure.[34] Society must focus on, prioritize ecological health, stability, as well as public health, education, housing, employment, etc. These cannot be treated as secondary or transactional to the capital accumulation process. Instead, all of the productive forces of society must be geared toward achieving the thriving of society and the individual, as well as the ecology. True democracy and the sovereignty of the people can only be attained under such a circumstance.[35]

The optimism that the world can achieve a thriving (classless) modern society, free of ethnic, and gender biases is derived from popular culture. In turning to popular culture as an epistemological source I rely on two separate (yet related) arguments. First, popular culture can be read as an indicator of public opinion/reasoning. In *The Politics of* Star Trek I make the following argument:

> In asking why the *Star Trek* franchise is so entertaining to so many, we are engaging public opinion at the deepest levels. The Federation, across all of *Star Trek*'s platforms, is a secular (at times anti-religion) interstellar institution that is classless, and predicated on the total absence of gender/ethnic biases. In this way the franchise is based on reason (i.e., full and total equality). Thus, *Star Trek*'s enduring popularity can/should be read as the broader public's adherence to reason and a rejection of pre-modernism (religion/aristocracy) (as well as post-modernism [i.e., critiques of reason]).[36]

The second reason I hold that popular culture is a reliable source of knowledge relates to the philosophizing of Georg Hegel and his theory of the absolute. This second theory motivated my book *The Absolute and* Star Trek[37]:

> How can we know the *absolute*?—through art.[38] The *absolute*, philosophized upon most saliently by Georg Hegel,[39] is the driving force behind history.[40] Classicist Henry Paolucci explains that "art" (along with religion and philosophy) "are in the end, for Hegel, 'moments' of *absolute spirit*."[41] Similarly, philosopher William Desmond, in *A Study of Hegel's Aesthetics: Art and the Absolute*, notes that "Art has an *absolute* dimension; indeed, it belongs together with religion and philosophy itself as one of the three highest modes of human meaning."[42] Consonant with Hegelian reasoning, my specific argument in this volume is that the broadcast iterations of *Star Trek* allow us to comprehend significant aspects of the absolute. Therefore, *Star Trek* is the highest of highbrow entertainment.[43]

Hence, the absolute (a fifth dimension where justice and other normative values emanate from) is understood through art, and the broadcast iterations of *Star Trek* (given their popularity) are a particularly good source of knowledge of justice (as determined by the Absolute). *Star Trek* (arguably) is popular precisely because it tracks the justice that inheres within the absolute. Philosophy Professor Jack Kaminsky, drawing explicitly on Hegel's theory of aesthetics, explains that "the artist tries to show men what kind of man would be the fullest expression of the Idea" (i.e., the Absolute).[44] Therefore, very plausibly, the artistic success of the *Star Trek* franchise (and its great popularity) is precisely due to the fact that it shows us *what kind of person/society would be the fullest expression of the Absolute*.

Analytic philosophy, whose adherents have historically ridiculed the idea of the absolute[45]—without positing any answers of their own for the movement of history[46]—is an obstacle to knowledge. Most specifically, art and the analyzing of the aesthetic are viewed by analytic philosophers as mainly outside of epistemology and ignorable as it relates to science. The humanities, in actuality, is of a piece with the physical sciences[47]—as they both *speculate* about the absolute, the latter about its manifestation in matter and energy, whereas the former (in its finer forms) is *speculation* about the absolute as it pertains to human affairs.[48] "Art may not have the precision of physics but, according to Hegel, it has as crucial a role in revealing to us an aspect of the [Absolute] Idea."[49] Because analytic philosophers reject the arts as a source of knowledge, this approach serves to block the truth—knowledge of the absolute (and justice) through art (chapter 1).

OVERVIEW

Humanity has gone through significant philosophical (political) turns (stoic and socratic). Without a coherent, universal conception of justice the next philosophical turn could be the dystopian (racist) Trump turn (chapter 2). The fact that super-wealthy capitalist elites—like Trump—

would turn to racism suggests that the current neoliberalist world itself is a dystopia (chapter 3). Without a justice framework that incorporates all of humanity, people have turned to identity, *grievance* politics to politically organize—itself a dangerous, dystopian turn (chapter 4). A political, philosophical failure of humanity (modernity) has been to limit the metaphysics debate to one between analytic philosophy and religion. Religious metaphysics portends a limited, flawed rights regime that facilitates injustice and repression (chapter 5). The *Star Trek* text allows us to gain an understanding of what a post-capitalist, communist politics, society would look like. Under communism there is no state (a repressive institution), but there is government—to help achieve the full potential of modernity, as well as oversee the implementation of the justice regime. A communist government would be based on a profound commitment to truth, social justice, and intellectual discovery. Lacking an entrenched elite/caste, with such normative commitments we can be assured that government will not devolve into a repressive state (chapter 6). In communist society art would be engaged in by all. Art would be a part of the process of intellectual discovery and speculation (chapter 7).

NOTES

1. Dan Levin, "'Justice' Prevails: Dictionary Picks 2018 Word of the Year," *New York Times*, December 18, 2018, A15.

2. Daniel Stedman Jones, *Masters of the Universe: Hayek, Friedman, and the Birth of Neoliberal Politics* (Princeton: Princeton University Press, 2012); Adam Kotsko, *Neoliberalism's Demons: On the Political Theology of Late Capital* (Stanford: Stanford University Press, 2018).

3. Christopher H. Achen, *Democracy for Realists: Why Elections Do Not Produce Responsive Government* (Princeton: Princeton University Press, 2017); Steven Levitsky and Daniel Ziblatt, *How Democracies Die* (New York: Crown, 2018); Dana Goldstein, "A More Perfect Civics Lesson? 'Democracy' Itself Is Up for Debate," *New York Times*, April 8, 2019, A1; Michael Tomasky, "America's Coming Oligarchy," *New York Times*, April 15, 2019, A23.

4. Timothy J. Sinclair, *The New Masters of Capital: American Bond Rating Agencies and the Politics of Creditworthiness* (Ithaca: Cornell University Press, 2014); Clyde W. Barrow, *Toward a Critical Theory of States: The Poulantzas-Miliband Debate after Globalization* (Albany: State University of New York Press, 2016); William Deringer, *Calculated Values: Finance, Politics, and the Quantitative Age* (Cambridge, MA: Harvard University Press, 2018).

5. Layna Mosley, *Global Capital and National Governments* (Cambridge: Cambridge University Press, 2003); Nick Wingfield and Patricia Cohen, "Let the Bidding Begin," *New York Times*, September 8, 2017, B1; David Streitfeld, "A Ruse or Brilliant Marketing by Amazon? Yes," *New York Times*, November 7, 2018, B4; Ben Casselman, "Nashville Leaves the Pack Behind," *New York Times*, December 17, 2018, B1; François Chesnais, *Finance Capital Today: Corporations and Banks in the Lasting Global Slump* (Chicago: Haymarket Books, 2018).

6. Jane L. Collins and Victoria Mayer, *Both Hands Tied: Welfare Reform and the Race to the Bottom in the Low-Wage Labor Market* (Chicago: University of Chicago Press, 2010); Kristin S. Seefedt and John D. Graham, *America's Poor and the Great Recession* (Bloomington: Indiana University Press, 2013); Richard Fausset, "Daring to Say No to

Big Oil," *New York Times*, February 5, 2019, B1; Lisa Friedman, "E.P.A.'s Reckoning Is a Rosier View of Air Pollution," *New York Times*, May 21, 2019, A1; Jacob S. Hacker, "Strong Economy, Worried Americans," *New York Times*, May 22, 2019, A21, and *The Great Risk Shift: The New Economic Insecurity and the Decline of the American Dream*, 2nd ed. (New York: Oxford University Press, 2019).

7. Liam Downey, *Inequality, Democracy, and the Environment* (New York: New York University Press, 2015); Paul Krugman, "The G.O.P. Goes Full Authoritarian," *New York Times*, December. 11, 2018, A26.

8. Ryan J. Barilleaux and Christopher S. Kelley, eds., *The Unitary Executive and the Modern Presidency* (College Station: Texas A&M University Press, 2010); Charlie Savage and Maggie Haberman, "An Advocate of Presidential Power Interests Trump for Attorney General," *New York Times*, December 7, 2018, A15; Peter Baker, "Trump's Insults End a Brief Civil Interlude," *New York Times*, December 8, 2018, A10; Emily Cochrane, "A Passive Congress Enables Trump to Use Pulpit to Continue His Shutdown Chatter," *New York Times*, December 25, 2018, A15; Charles Blow, "An Imperial Presidency?" *New York Times*, May 13, 2019, A19.

9. Terry H. Anderson, *Bush's Wars* (New York: Oxford University Press, 2013); Geoffroy de Lagasnerie, *The Art of Revolt: Snowden, Assange, Manning* (Stanford: Stanford University Press, 2017).

10. Jean Elshtain, *Just War Against Terror: The Burden of American Power in a Violent World* (New York: Basic Books, 2008); Sheryl Gay Stolberg, "Senate Rejects Bipartisan Challenge to Post–9/11 Presidential War Powers," *New York Times*, September 14, 2017, A15; Satvinder S. Juss, ed., *Beyond Human Rights and the War on Terror* (New York: Routledge, 2018); Saher Selod, *Forever Suspect: Racialized Surveillance of Muslim Americans in the War on Terror* (Newark: Rutgers University Press, 2018); Zolan Kanno-Youngs, "Cyberwarfare Is Top Threat Facing U.S., Nielsen Says," *New York Times*, March 19, 2019, A17.

11. Alexander Burns, "Pushing Someone Rich, Trump Offers Himself," *New York Times*, June 17, 2015, A16.

12. Ali Rattansi, *Racism: A Very Short Introduction* (New York: Oxford University Press, 2007); Michael D. Shear, "Trump Imposes New Travel Ban on 7 Countries," *New York Times*, September 25, 2017, A1.

13. Peter Baker, "Trump Calls Emergency, Defying Congress," *New York Times*, February 16, 2019, A1; Helene Cooper, "Defense Chief Plans to Use War Funds to Build Wall," *New York Times*, May 11, 2019, A16.

14. Katrin Bennhold, "Veering to Germany's Political Extremes," *New York Times*, October 13, 2018, A4; Matt Stevens, Megan Specia and Patrick Kingsley, "Clinton Warns Europe of Peril of Open Doors," *New York Times*, November 23, 2018, A1; Katrin Bennhold, "German Far-Right Group: Neo-Nazis Rebranded," *New York Times*, December 28, 2018, A1; Jose Pedro Zuquete, *The Identitarians: The Movement Against Globalism and Islam in Europe* (South Bend, IN: University of Notre Dame Press, 2018); Nellie Bowles, "As Birthrates Fall, Fearing 'Replacement' on Far Right," *New York Times*, March 19, 2019, A8; Steven Erlanger, "Far Right is Seen Making Inroads as Europe Votes," *New York Times*, May 27, 2019, A1.

15. John Sides, Michael Tesler, and Lynn Vavreck, *Identity Crisis: The 2016 Presidential Campaign and the Battle for the Meaning of America* (Princeton: Princeton University Press, 2018).

16. Joseph E. Stiglitz, *Globalization and Its Discontents Revisited: Anti-Globalization in the Era of Trump* (New York: W.W. Norton, 2017); Peter S. Goodman, "Chief of W.T.O. Worries about Its Role as Peacekeeper as a Trade War Brews," *New York Times*, March 24, 2018, A9; Steven Erlanger, "Is U.S. Foreign Policy Reverting the World to a Dark 'Jungle'?" *New York Times*, September 23, 2018, A8; Ana Swanson and Jim Tankersley, "As Trump Moves to End Trade War with China, Business Asks: Was It Worth It?," *New York Times*, March 5, 2019, B1.

17. Mark Landler, "Trump Leaves U.S. and China on Tip of New Cold War," *New York Times*, September 20, 2018, A1; Edward Wong and Alan Rappeport, "U.S. and

China Push Nations to Pick a Side," *New York Times*, November 22, 2018, A1; Daisuke Wakabayashi and Alan Rappeport, "Arrest of a Top Huawei Executive Further Strains U.S.-China Ties," *New York Times*, December 6, 2018, A1; Mark Landler and Edward Wong, "Bolton Vows Bigger U.S. Role in Africa, but Goal Is Countering China's Sway," *New York Times*, December 14, 2018, A11; Maria Abi-Habib, "India's Military, Ailing and Poor, Nears Its Brink," *New York Times*, March 4, 2019, A1.

18. Nicholas Fandos and Sharon LaFraniere, "Two Reports on Meddling: Choose Your Own Verdict," *New York Times*, April 28, 2018, A14.

19. Andrew E. Kramer and Megan Specia, "The Risks to Russia, China and Europe as the U.S. Scraps a Nuclear Deal," *New York Times*, February 2, 2019, A9; David E. Sanger and William J. Broad, "U.S. Plans to End Nuclear Accord Signed by Russia," *New York Times*, February 2, 2019, A1; Andrew E. Kramer, "A Day after U.S. Leaves Nuclear Pact Russia Announces It Will Do the Same," *New York Times*, February 3, 2019, A7; Sabrina Tavernise, "A New Country for Conflict Resolution Experts: The U.S.," *New York Times*, February 5, 2019, A12; Alexandra Stevenson, "Xi Rallies His People as Trade War Intensifies," *New York Times*, May 22, 2019, A7; Keith Bradsher, "Trade Wedge for China: Its Minerals," *New York Times*, May 24, 2019, B1.

20. George A. Gonzalez, *Energy, the Modern State, and the American World System* (Albany: State University of New York Press, 2018); Li Yuan, "Some in China Fear Severing Ties with U.S.," *New York Times*, May 15, 2019, A1.

21. Elizabeth Kolbert, *The Sixth Extinction: An Unnatural History* (New York: Henry Holt, 2014); Naomi Oreskes and Erik M. Conway, *The Collapse of Western Civilization: A View from the Future* (New York: Columbia University Press, 2014); Justin Gillis, "Scientists Sound Alarm on Climate," *New York Times*, March 18, 2014, D1, and "Study Warns of a Perilous Climate Shift within Decades," *New York Times*, March 23, 2016, A11; Anthony D. Barnosky, *Dodging Extinction: Power, Food, Money, and the Future of Life on Earth* (Berkeley: University of California Press, 2016); William B. Gail, "A New Dark Age Looms," *New York Times*, April 19, 2016, A27; John Schwartz, "400," *New York Times*, October 4, 2016, D3, "'Like a Terror Movie': How Changing Climate Will Multiply Disasters," *New York Times*, November 20, 2018, A11, and "Will We Survive Climate Change?," *New York Times*, November 20, 2018, D7; Abrahm Lustgarten, "Fuel to the Fire," *New York Times Magazine*, November 25, 2018, 42; Paul Krugman, "The Depravity of Climate-Change Denial," *New York Times*, November 27, 2018, A22; Carl Zimmer, "Earth's Near-Death Experience," *New York Times*, December 11, 2018, D3; John Schwartz, "In NOAA's Forecast, Flooding 'Worse Than Anything We've Seen in Recent Years,'" *New York Times*, March 22, 2019, A18; Michelle Cottle, "Where's Your Climate Plan, Mr. McConnell?," *New York Times*, March 27, 2019, A22; Eric Lipton, "Interior Nominee Helped Quash Pesticide Report," *New York Times*, March 27, 2019, A1; Carl Zimmer, "The Lost History of Biosphere 2," *New York Times*, March 31, 2019, SR1; Stephen Nash, "The Empty Forests of Vietnam," *New York Times*, April 7, 2019, TR1; Jennifer Vineyard, "Spoiler: The Villains in 'Our Planet' Are Humans," *New York Times*, April 9, 2019, C2; Marc Santora, "Poles Fear for Ancient Woodlands Despite Court Action," *New York Times*, April 10, 2019, A8; Brad Plumer, "Wildlife Facing Extinction Risk All Over Globe," *New York Times*, May 7, 2019, A1; Mitch Smith and John Schwartz, "It's Bad, It's Real, Just Don't Call It Climate Change," *New York Times*, May 16, 2019, A10.

22. Ruth Whippman,"We're All in Sales Now," *New York Times*, November 25, 2018, SR1; David Leonhardt, "When C.E.O.s Cared about America," *New York Times*, December 3, 2018, A27, and "A C.E.O. Scared for His Country," *New York Times*, April 1, 2019, A21.

23. Peter Singer, *Marx: A Very Short Introduction* (New York: Oxford University Press, 2001); Gareth Stedman Jones, *Karl Marx: Greatness and Illusion* (Cambridge: Cambridge University Press, 2016).

24. David Harvey, *A Brief History of Neoliberalism* (New York: Oxford University Press, 2007).

25. Dan Levin, "Billionaire Roulette," *New York Times*, November 11, 2018, ST1; Tim Wu, *The Curse of Bigness: Antitrust in the New Gilded Age* (New York: Columbia Global Reports, 2018).

26. Peter S. Goodman, "U.S. and Global Economies Slipping in Unison," *New York Times*, August 24, 2008, A1; David Harvey, *Seventeen Contradictions and the End of Capitalism* (New York: Oxford University Press, 2014), and *Marx, Capital, and the Madness of Economic Reason* (New York: Oxford University Press, 2017).

27. V. I. Lenin, *Imperialism: The Highest Stage of Capitalism* (New York: Pluto, 1996 [1917]); Christopher Read, *Lenin: A Revolutionary Life* (New York: Routledge, 2005).

28. Mary Elizabeth Gallagher, *Contagious Capitalism: Globalization and the Politics of Labor in China* (Princeton: Princeton University Press, 2005); Kelly Sims Gallagher, *China Shifts Gears: Automakers, Oil, Pollution, and Development* (Cambridge, MA: MIT Press, 2006); John Markoff, "When Apple Was Homegrown," *New York Times*, December 17, 2018, B6; Keith Bradsher, "Rethinking China's Role as the World's Factory," *New York Times*, April 6, 2019, A1.

29. Landler, "Trump Leaves U.S. and China on Tip of New Cold War"; Wong and Rappeport, "U.S. and China Push Nations to Pick a Side"; Li Yuan "Retooling China, from the Bottom Up," *New York Times*, July 5, 2018, B1; Keith Bradsher, "2 Possible Paths Emerge in China Trade War," *New York Times*, August 9, 2018, B1; H. Bruce Franklin, *Crash Course: From the Good War to the Forever War* (Newark: Rutgers University Press, 2018); Keith Bradsher and Ana Swanson, "China Digs In on Subsidies as Trade Deal Stalls," *New York Times*, May 13, 2019, B1; Adam Satariano, Raymond Zhong, and Daisuke Wakabayashi, "Putting the Squeeze on Huawei," *New York Times*, May 15, 2019, A16.

30. Adrian Parr, *The Wrath of Capital: Neoliberalism and Climate Change Politics* (New York: Columbia University Press, 2013); George A. Gonzalez, *American Empire and the Canadian Oil Sands* (New York: Palgrave Macmillan, 2016); Kendra Pierre-Louis, "U.S. Climate Study Has Grim Warning of Economic Risks," *New York Times*, November 24, 2018, A1; Somini Sengupta, "Coal Endangers a Planet Unable to Stop Using It," *New York Times*, November 25, 2018, A1; Coral Davenport and Lisa Friedman, "From Very Beginning, Broad Effort to Loosen the Rules on Pollution," *New York Times*, November 27, 2018, A12; Ernesto Londoño and Lisa Friedman, "Brazil Backs Out of Holding Climate Change Meeting for U.N.," *New York Times*, November 29, 2018, A4; Lisa Friedman, "E.P.A. Will Ease Path to New Coal Plants," *New York Times*, December 5, 2018, B3; Kendra Pierre-Louis, "Emissions Surge, Hastening Perils across the Globe," *New York Times*, December 6, 2018, A1; Brad Plumer and Lisa Friedman, "Trump Has Allies on Fossil Fuels," *New York Times*, December 11, 2018, A1; David Montgomery and Annie Karni, "President Lauds Curbs to Energy Regulations," *New York Times*, May 15, 2019, A16.

31. David Leonhardt, "Companies Behind a Power Grab," *New York Times*, December 10, 2018, A27; Catie Edmondson, "G.O.P. Scorns Judges' Rating By Bar Group," *New York Times*, December 12, 2018, A1; Hiroko Tabuchi, "The Oil Industry's Covert Campaign to Rewrite American Car Emissions Rules," *New York Times*, December 13, 2018. Web; Nick Corasaniti, "Democrats, Flush with Power, Try to Grab More," *New York Times*, December 14, 2018, A1; Julie Turkewitz and Coral Davenport, "Leader of Interior Dept. Resigns Under Cloud of Ethics Inquiries," *New York Times*, December 16, 2018, A1; Paul Krugman, "Conservatism's Monstrous Endgame," *New York Times*, December 18, 2018, A22.

32. Clyde W. Barrow, *Critical Theories of the State* (Madison: University of Wisconsin Press, 1993), 17; Barrow explains that "corporations emerged as the dominant economic institutions in capitalist societies by the end of the nineteenth century." He goes on to note that as early as the late 1920s "the bulk of U.S. economic activity, whether measured in terms of assets, profits, employment, investment, market shares, or research and development, was concentrated in the fifty largest financial institutions and five hundred largest nonfinancial corporations." Ibid. Also see, Thomas Piketty, *Capital in the Twenty-First Century*, trans. Arthur Goldhammer (Cambridge, MA: Bel-

knap Press, 2014); Patricia Cohen, "Study Finds Global Wealth Is Flowing to the Richest," *New York Times*, January 19, 2015, B6; Gerry Mullany, "World's 8 Richest Have as Much Wealth as Bottom Half, Oxfam Says," *New York Times*, January 16, 2017. Web.

Political Scientists Jeffrey A. Winters and Benjamin I. Page, writing in 2009, hold that "it is now appropriate to . . . think about the possibility of *extreme* political inequality, involving great political influence by a very small number of extremely wealthy individuals." They go on to add that "we argue that it is useful to think about the U.S. political system in terms of oligarchy." Jeffrey A. Winters and Benjamin I. Page, "Oligarchy in the United States," *Perspectives on Politics*, Vol. 7, No. 4, 2009, 744, emphasis in original; also see Paul Krugman, "Oligarchy, American Style," *New York Times*, November 4, 2011, A31, and "The Undeserving Rich," *New York Times*, January 20, 2014, A17; Jeffrey A. Winters, *Oligarchy* (New York: Cambridge University Press, 2011); Shaila Dewan and Robert Gebeloff, "One Percent, Many Variations," *New York Times*, January 15, 2012, A1; David Leonhardt, "All for the 1 percent, 1 percent for All," *New York Times*, May 4, 2014, MM23; Nicholas Kristof, "An Idiot's Guide to Inequality," *New York Times*, July 24, 2014, A27; Anna Bernasek, "The Typical Household, Now Worth a Third Less," *New York Times*, July 27, 2014, BU6; Neil Irwin, "Economic Expansion for Everyone? Not Anymore," *New York Times*, September 27, 2014, B1; Robert Frank, "Another Widening Gap: The Haves vs. the Have-Mores," *New York Times*, November 16, 2014, BU4; Peter Eavis, "It's Never Been Easier to Be a C.E.O., and the Pay Keeps Rising," *New York Times*, May 26, 2019, BU4.

33. Sunaina Marr Maira, *The 9/11 Generation: Youth, Rights, and Solidarity in the War on Terror* (New York: New York University Press, 2016).

34. Tom Rockmore, *Marx's Dream: From Capitalism to Communism* (Chicago: University of Chicago Press, 2018).

35. Leslie Holmes, *Communism: A Very Short Introduction* (New York: Oxford University Press, 2009); Bini Adamczak, *Communism for Kids* (Cambridge, MA: MIT Press, 2017).

36. George A. Gonzalez, *The Politics of* Star Trek*: Justice, War, and the Future* (New York: Palgrave Macmillan, 2015), 1–2.

37. George A. Gonzalez, *The Absolute and* Star Trek (New York: Palgrave Macmillan, 2017), vii.

38. William Maker, ed., *Hegel and Aesthetics* (Albany: State University of New York Press, 2000); Kirk Pillow, *Sublime Understanding: Aesthetic Reflection in Kant and Hegel* (Cambridge, MA: MIT Press, 2000); Paul Gordon, *Art as the Absolute: Art's Relation to Metaphysics in Kant, Fichte, Schelling, Hegel, and Schopenhauer* (New York: Bloomsbury Academic, 2015).

39. Donald Phillip Verene, *Hegel's Absolute: An Introduction to Reading the Phenomenology of Spirit* (Albany: State University New York Press, 2007); Stephen Houlgate, *Hegel's "Phenomenology of Spirit": A Reader's Guide* (New York: Bloomsbury Academic, 2013); Brady Bowman, *Hegel and the Metaphysics of Absolute Negativity* (Cambridge: Cambridge University Press, 2015).

40. Robert L. Perkins, ed., *History and System: Hegel's Philosophy of History* (Albany: State University of New York, 1984); Will Dudley, ed., *Hegel and History* (Albany: State University of New York Press, 2009).

41. Henry Paolucci, "Introduction" in *Hegel: On the Arts*, Henry Paolucci, ed., 2nd ed. (Smyrna, DE: Griffon House, 2001), xix, emphasis added.

42. William Desmond, *Art and the Absolute: A Study of Hegel's Aesthetics* (Albany: State University of New York Press, 1986), xii, emphasis added.

43. Lawrence Levine, *Highbrow/Lowbrow: The Emergence of Cultural Hierarchy in America* (Cambridge, MA: Harvard University Press, 1990); Jason T. Eberl and Kevin S. Decker, eds., Star Trek *and Philosophy: The Wrath of Kant* (Chicago: Open Court, 2008).

44. Jack Kaminsky, *Hegel on Art: An Interpretation of Hegel's Aesthetics* (Albany: State University of New York Press, 1962), 29.

45. Hans-Johann Glock, *What Is Analytic Philosophy?* (New York: Cambridge University Press, 2008), 117–21.

46. Ibid., chap. 4.

47. Siân Ede, *Art and Science* (New York: I. B. Tauris, 2005); Martin Kemp, *Seen | Unseen: Art, Science, and Intuition from Leonardo to the Hubble Telescope* (New York: Oxford University Press, 2006); Steven Connor, "Doing without Art," *New Literary History*, vol. 42, no. 1: 53–69; Bence Nanay, *Aesthetics as Philosophy of Perception* (New York: Oxford University Press, 2016).

48. E.g., Rebecca Solnit, "Bird by Bird," *New York Times Magazine*, December 7, 2014, MM13; Adam Frank, "Is a Climate Disaster Inevitable?" *New York Times*, January 18, 2015, SR6.

49. Kaminsky, *Hegel on Art*, 21.

ONE

Analytic Philosophy as Anti-Justice

The analytic philosophy *turn* was a turn away from justice. Now with Alex Rosenberg's *How History Gets Things Wrong* analytic philosophy is turning *against* justice. In this chapter I counter analytic philosophy with the thinking of Georg Hegel (1770–1831)—who argued that normative values metaphysically exist in the Absolute.[1] I further rely on Karl Marx's argument that history (the absolute) operates as a *progressive dialectic*—whereby humanity through a series of revolutions is evolving toward *justice* (an ideal modern classless society free of ethnic and gender biases).[2] Consonant with the thinking of American Trotskyists[3] (followers of the Russian Revolutionary leader Leon Trotsky) the creators of the *Star Trek* text depict the progressive dialectic as centered in the United States.

ANALYTIC PHILOSOPHY AS ANTI-JUSTICE

A singular dogma is at the center of analytic philosophy: knowledge has to be iterative, timeless, indisputably verifiable, and ultimately predicable.[4] In the end analytic philosophy can be read more so as rank propaganda for the physical sciences than an actual philosophy—as the analytic philosophers' criteria for knowledge are tailor made to equate knowledge with the laws of physics (a kind of tautology). Indeed, analytic philosophers consider themselves to be adjuncts to the physical sciences.[5] It should be noted that this philosophical turn to science in the American scene occurred under immense pressure from the McCarthyism of the 1950s and into the 1960s—where the philosophical, scholarly treatment of justice was deemed to be politically suspect (dangerous).[6] American political science during this period also became hyperempirical—with a dogmatic emphasis on the iterative (e.g., voting) as solely constituting knowledge.[7]

With philosophy and political science eliding justice both have been rendered feckless and demoralized.[8] In political science politics is reduced to "who gets what, when and how"[9]—an idea that propels rational choice theory.[10] Thus, the political is nothing more than the acute manifestation of self-centeredness, selfishness, and even corruption. When John Rawls advocated for justice he did so from a perspective of people as fundamentally self-regarding. So Rawls holds justice—fairness is putatively rational—desirable for the self-concerned person because anyone can become poor, disadvantaged, etc. Therefore, for Rawls there is no imperative for justice—other than the individual's fear of falling victim to unemployment, poverty, and discrimination.[11]

The height of philosophical cynicism is Richard Rorty's notion of *intersubjective agreement* (or neopragmatism).[12] Rorty asserts that while justice doesn't exist as a metaphysic, people invariably hold subjective concepts of justice. Two key points can be deduced from Rorty's intersubjective agreement argument. First, arguments made about justice can in most cases be reduced to self-interested politics under the guise or pretense of justice. Thus, there are no fundamental truths to justice claims—again, mostly (only) selfishness masquerading as justice. The second key point following from the idea of intersubjective agreement is that society is composed of such agreement. Hence, social peace/stability is derived exclusively from sufficient intersubjective agreement. Importantly, the content of the agreement doesn't matter only the degree of agreement. Without sufficient agreement, society breaks down. The obvious point is that for Rorty's formulation it doesn't matter if a society's intersubjective agreement is based on white supremacy, vilification of minorities, slavery, anti-Semitism, and so forth. The philosopher's role is solely to identify the content of such agreements.

The assault on the very idea of justice takes clear form in analytic philosopher Alex Rosenberg's recent tirade against history—published under the title *How History Gets Things Wrong*. Rosenberg's critique is not directed at history, per se, but people's notion of justice, as informed by popular historical understanding. For instance, people consider slavery to be unjust, immoral. Following from this they intuitively consider it illegal. The legality or illegality of slavery (in the American mind) was settled by the U.S. Civil War. An example of this reasoning in action is depicted in *Blue Bloods* (2009 to present) television episode "Trust" (2018). Jaime Reagan (a police Sargent) confronts a small shop owner over the nonpayment of employees and invokes the Civil War in making the seemingly obvious point that slavery is illegal, immoral.

Rather cynically, Rosenberg would likely point out that the idea that slavery was ended by the American Civil War is empirically false, as slavery in prisons is still Constitutional (according to the terms of the thirteenth amendment). The true aim of Rosenberg's critique, however, is not that people get history wrong (in spite of the title of his book), but, again, that people hew to concepts of justice. (He simply exploits the idea that people's notions of justice are invariably informed by an understanding of history that by necessity elide particular, specific facts.) This is not to condone the falsification of history, but more on this below. Rosenberg's specific critique is that people hold to concepts of justice and such concepts or beliefs are on balance pernicious/destructive. Again, using history as a in-stand for justice Rosenberg makes the following sweeping, almost astounding assertion: "Stories historians tell are deeply implicated in more misery and death than probably any other aspect of human culture."[13] Not imperialism, not militarism, not poverty, not ecological destruction, but histories that inform our concepts of justice are "deeply implicated in more misery and death." Consonant with Rorty's intersubjective agreement position Rosenberg holds that histories (i.e., justice claims) are solely politics by another means: "Many disputes between peoples are intractable owning to the histories each side tells itself." Significantly, Rosenberg goes on to give the example of the Israeli-Palestinian conflict as a product of competing (presumably profoundly flawed) histories as the source of the conflict, and not the fact that the Palestinians were massively displaced and are serially oppressed by the Israeli state.[14]

What is the most glaring and telling aspect of Rosenberg's argumentation is that he points exclusively to retrograde examples to justify his assault on history (popularly understood):

> The xenophobia, racism, and patriarchy that ruled long before the advent of the nation-state were already clothed in histories of who did what to whom. The nation-state, when it arrived, was just a more efficient means to raise the death toll of narratives.

What about historical narratives that promote fairness and equality?, such as those (for example) related to the American Revolutionary War, the fight against fascism, the Civil Rights movement, anticolonialism, etc. Rosenberg invokes science to hold that on balance history, or justice claims, are bad for humanity: "evolutionary anthropologists know enough about human cultural evolution to be confident that most histories have motivated and continue to motivate people and peoples to take from—or refuse to share with—others." Typical of Rosenberg's one-sided argumentation he only invokes the Old Testament to justify his position that history is a "vehicle of in-group bonding and out-group enmity."[15] What to make of the historiography in the American *Declaration of Independence* that leads to the momentous conclusion that "All Men are Created Equal"?

With Rosenberg, analytic philosophy comes full circle. The initial position of analytic philosophy was that justice claims were irrelevant to knowledge, which is equated with science and the laws of physics. Now, science is being deployed to argue that not only are justice claims inherently false (based on flawed histories), but such claims are profoundly dangerous and the source of virtually all of humanity's social, political ills.

Rosenberg's argument that history (as politics) must be abandoned is in line with the Nazi project. In *The Absolute and* Star Trek, I outline the following:

> The Nazi project, I would argue, was specifically geared toward negating the progressive dialectic (the "Victory of Faith"[16]), or, more specifically, drowning the progressive dialectic in blood and suppressing it through a sustained regime of terror and violence. The Nazis' hateful attitude toward the progressive dialectic was manifest in its venom (to put it mildly) toward Marxism, Bolshevism, and, Jews, more broadly[17]—who were viewed as the intellectual bearers of the progressive dialectic.[18]

Thus, ideologically speaking, the Nazis sought to destroy or suppress progressive politics, progressive histories (humanity as evolving toward ideal, universal justice and fairness), or the *progressive dialectic*.[19]

This understanding of the Nazi project is in a certain sense confirmed by the Amazon Prime series *The Man in the High Castle* (2015 to present). The series presents an alternative history, whereby the Germans and Japanese won World War Two and occupy and control the United States as a result. The 2018 season focuses in particular on American politics under the control of the Nazis. Set in the early 1960s, the Nazis decide to institute a new American politics and history. They do so through the slogan of "Year Zero"—the idea that U.S. history begins in the early 1960s, under a Nazi ideological regime. As part of this policy/program, the American past (history) must be suppressed or forgotten. Symbols emotive of liberty, equality, and fairness are systemically destroyed (the Statue of Liberty, the Liberty Bell).

The Nazis in *The Man in the High Castle* want to replace the progressive aspects of American history with *Bullshit*. Here I'm referring to Harry Frankfurt's argument that in the modern context something he labels "bullshit" has been created—a new category of epistemology (knowledge).[20] Bullshit can be deemed antiknowledge. The categories of truth and lies are both predicated on accurate empirical claims. Lies presume the existence valid of empiricism—but misrepresent reality. Those that bullshit are uninterested in the truth and seek to create or impose completely false narratives—entirely disconnected from history, facts. The actual Nazis were seemingly the first to engage in a policy of Bullshit with their Big Lie technique—the repeating (through modern means of communication) of politically useful fantasies over and over again. In doing so, the public comes to acquiesce in the face of such repeatedly propagated fantasies and myopia—the Aryan Race, the Jewish Conspiracy, etc. Frankfurt's 2005 book was ostensibly aimed at the Bullshit (Iraq's weapons of mass destruction) concocted by the Bush administration, with the help of the *New York Times* and other national, international media, which paved the way for the 2003 invasion and conquest of Iraq.

Importantly, Rosenberg fails to distinguish Bullshit from actual history. He specifically points to the German far right argument that the country was "stabbed in the back" during World War One.[21] Such bullshit is used by Rosenberg to argue that all historical narratives are marked by such extreme falseness.

Rosenberg wants to replace America's history (including its progressive elements) with the bullshit of "science": "even when we come to recognize [history's] harmful effects, we continue to crave the sensation it produces. And we'll never be comfortable with the only medication that can block its harmful effects—science."[22] As noted above, Rosenberg uses the bullshit of *geneticism* (the idea that genes drive human behavior) to hold that our interest in history is determined by genes—in a manner that is perniciously self-centered. People's interest in history is specifically derived from their interest in improving society and engaging a fairer, more just politics.[23] This is depicted in *Star Trek: The Next Generation*. When a political witch hunt erupts on the *Enterprise*, Captain Picard is steeled in his opposition to the hysteria by his knowledge of history:

> Five hundred years ago, military officers would upend a drum on the battlefield sit at it and dispense summary justice. Decisions were quick, punishments severe, appeals denied. Those who came to a drumhead were doomed. ("The Drumhead" 1991)

More broadly, in the *Next Generation* pilot ("Farpoint Station" 1987) when the omnipotent Q condemns humanity based on its violent history, Picard objects, arguing that humanity is well aware of this history and is determined not to repeat it. (Picard: "That nonsense is centuries behind us!" "Even as far back as . . . we had begun to make rapid progress.") Humans regularly refer to history to understand/analyze/improve the present. Thus, human consciousness is figuratively a product of history.

This is not to deny that venal, corrupt interests seek to misrepresent, distort history—use it for nefarious ends, and to institute regimes of repression. Nevertheless, Rosenberg's idea that we should abandon history as a politics and replace it with science is a meaningless suggestion. What does science mean in this instance?—a fixation on fact, without any regard for meaning? Again, this has no actual content—as it is impossible to separate facts from their social or political meaning.[24]

Rosenberg's seeming intent is to stigmatize progressive history and politics. He equates such history with *bullshit* (the German far right "stab in the back" position). Rosenberg holds we should abandon progressive politics and history in favor of *science*—an empty-headed idea, and a complete misuse of the prestige (strong social standing) of the physical sciences.

Man in the High Castle shows the making of a Nazi propaganda film where workers are dismantling, destroying the Lincoln statue of the Lincoln Memorial ("Sabra" 2018). This is of particular significance because while Lincoln was an American president, as the leader of the Northern victory over the Southern slavocracy he is a figure of worldwide saliency. Arguably, Lincoln is the person most credited in the modern era with the defeat of feudalism in the West, and the concomitant triumph of progressive modernism.[25] The editors of the volume *The Global Lincoln* explain that "Lincoln's global celebrity lies in . . . his resolute defense of popular government and free labor."[26] As I explain in the next section, the personage of Abraham Lincoln is a salient figure in the progressive dialectic.

THE PROGRESSIVE DIALECTIC OF *STAR TREK*

The *progressive dialectic* was initially identified by Karl Marx, and later acted upon by Leon Trotsky. The progressive dialectic is artistically represented in the "United Federation of Planets"—the fictional interstellar political entity in *Star Trek* which humans lead. The failure to speculate about the *absolute* and pursue the *progressive dialectic* is to precipitate disaster for humanity. *Star Trek* in artistically conveying the progressive dialectic makes the specific argument that if humanity/civilization is to survive/thrive that capitalist values have to be abandoned and neoliberalism has to be replaced.

STAR TREK AND CAPITALISM

Star Trek explicitly rejects capitalism in the *Next Generation* episode "The Neutral Zone" (1988). A wealthy businessman, named "Ralph Offenhouse," from the late-twentieth century is revived from a cryogenic chamber floating in space. (*Next Generation* takes place in the twenty-fourth century.) Upon being awoken, Ralph explains that "I have a substantial portfolio. It's critical I check on it." Later, he adds "I have to phone Geneva right away about my accounts. The interest alone could be enough to buy even this ship." Ralph dons an attitude of arrogance, entitlement, and authority. He tells Captain Picard "I demand you see me." When Picard tries to put Ralph off by referring to the sensitive situation the ship is dealing with at the time, Ralph retorts "I'm sure that whatever it is seems very important to you. My situation is far more critical." Ralph condescends to the Captain: "It is simply that I have more to protect than a man in your position could possibly imagine. No offense, but a military career has never been considered upwardly mobile." Picard, losing his patience, informs Ralph that his value system (and attitude) is misplaced and disdained in the current epoch:

Picard: A lot has changed in three hundred years. People are no longer obsessed with the accumulation of "things." We have eliminated hunger, want, the need for possessions. We have grown out of our infancy.

Ralph: You've got it wrong. It's never been about "possessions"—it's about power.[27]

Picard: Power to do what?

Ralph: To control your life, your destiny.

Picard: That kind of control is an illusion.

Chastened, Ralph asks "There's no trace of my money—my office is gone—what will I do? How will I live?" Picard explains "Those material needs no longer exist." Ralph, invoking the values of the late twentieth century, responds by asking: "Then what's the challenge?" Picard, seemingly outlining the values of twenty-fourth-century Earth, retorts: "To improve yourself . . . enrich yourself. Enjoy it, Mister Offenhouse."

Similarly, in the *Deep Space Nine* episode "In the Cards" (1997), Jake Sisko exclaims "I'm Human, I don't have any money." Nog, a Ferengi—an alien race that operates on the profit-motive—is critical of twenty-fourth-century humanity: "It's not my fault that your species decided to abandon currency-based economics in favor of some philosophy of self-enhancement." Shifting humanity's (America's) values away from "currency-based economics" and toward a "philosophy of self-enhancement" mirrors Karl Marx's point that in moving from capitalism to communism society would go "From each according to his ability, to each according to his needs!"—i.e., communist politics would focus on "the all-around development of the individual."[28] Or as Jake told Nog: "There's nothing wrong with our philosophy. We work to better ourselves and the rest of humanity."

Indicative of how humans in the twenty-fourth century have undergone a profound paradigm shift in values and outlook, Quark, a Ferengi who traveled back to mid-twentieth-century Earth (more specifically, the United States), concludes from his dealings with humans (Americans) in this epoch, that "these humans, they're not like the ones from the [twenty-fourth century] Federation. They're crude, gullible and greedy."[29] Marx offers a consonant rebuke of the cultural/social ethos of capitalists: "Contempt for theory, art, history, and for man as an end in himself . . . is the real, conscious standpoint, the virtue of the man of money."[30]

Therefore, *Star Trek* takes the Enlightenment to its logical conclusion—namely, that modernity; science; reason can serve as the basis for a peaceful; highly productive; and thriving world.[31] *Star Trek* is optimistic insofar as arguing that as global society accepts modernity, reason, and science (i.e., the progressive dialectic) humans will collectively achieve a higher plane of intelligence, knowledge, and emotional maturity. (An optimism shared by Marx: in "communist society . . . the all-round development of the individual" will be achieved.[32]) This higher plane of existence, however, requires the overthrow of the neoliberal order.

NEOLIBERALISM

To the American Revolutionary War (see below), the U.S. Civil War (see below), and the American fight against Fascism (original series—"City on the Edge of Forever" 1967), *Star Trek* adds to America's revolutionary "moments" with the Bell Uprising. Aired in 1995, "Past Tense" is centered on this fictional uprising. The characters Sisko, Bashir, and Dax are accidentally sent back to 2024 San Francisco, where, like in "City on the Edge of Forever," they alter Earth's history for the worse. Upon being beamed to the past, Sisko and Bashir are separated from Dax. Without any identification (or money) Sisko and Bashir are forcibly interned in an urban detainment camp for the poor and dispossessed. It is described in script notes as follows:

> Sisko and Bashir ENTER a street lined by dirty, dilapidated buildings, with boarded up windows and impromptu campsites set up in the doorways and stairwells. It's a sharp contrast to the relatively clean city outside. The street is crowded with poorly dressed homeless men, women, and children, of all ages and races, many standing in a long food line.[33]

Sisko, who is knowledgeable about twenty-first-century Earth, explains that "by the early twenty-twenties there was a place like this in every major city in the United States."

> **Bashir** asks: Why are these people in here? Are they criminals?
>
> **Sisko**: No. People with criminal records weren't allowed in the Sanctuary Districts.
>
> **Bashir**: Then what did they do to deserve this?
>
> **Sisko**: Nothing. They're just people. People without jobs or places to live.
>
> **Bashir**: So they get put in here?
>
> **Sisko**: Welcome to the twenty-first century.

Writing in the mid-1990s about internment camps for the poor and homeless being in place in every major American city within thirty years is an explicit critique of the neoliberal project, which was well established by the 1990s.[34] Neoliberalism, whose proponents prioritize the free movement of capital, goods, and services, has been devastating to numerous U.S. urban centers, particularly in the former industrial American heartland.[35] Cities like Detroit[36] and Cleveland[37]—which were global centers of industrial production—have been hollowed out as the U.S. manufacturing base has been shifted to cheap wage venues in the U.S. South, Mexico, China, etc.[38] One of the displaced residents of the San Francisco Sanctuary District explains that "I used to be a Plant Manager at ChemTech Industries." The result has been pronounced urban decay in once wealthy and prosperous cities,[39] where a substantial homeless population is an enduring phenomenon.[40]

Moreover, the Great Recession of 2008 has caused persistently high unemployment.[41] A historically destabilizing factor of capitalism is the tendency of capital equipment (i.e., technology) to replace labor.[42] In a 2012 op-ed piece in the *New York Times*, Princeton economist, Paul Krugman holds "there's no question that in some high-profile industries, technology is displacing workers of all, or almost all, kinds."[43] A Sanctuary District resident explains that "I came to San Francisco to work in a brewery but they laid a bunch of us off when they got some new equipment and so I ended up here." Another of the characters in "Past Tense" notes that "right now jobs are hard to come by . . . what with the economy and all." The former plant manager plaintively explains: "Most of us agreed to live here [in the San Francisco Sanctuary District] because they promised us jobs. I don't know about you, but I haven't been on any job interviews lately. And neither has anyone else. They've forgotten about us."

The overriding need to pursue societal justice (i.e., topple neoliberalism/capitalism) is made clear in "Past Tense." While in the Sanctuary District (in 2024 San Francisco) Sisko intervenes into a fight, which results in the death of one Gabriel Bell—the would-be leader of the Bell Uprising. Like the victory of the Nazis in World War Two ("City on the Edge of Forever"), this erases the entire history of the Federation. Meanwhile, back in the twenty-fourth century, all that remains of the original timeline is the ship (the *Defiant*) that beamed Sisko, Bashir, and Dax to the past. Uncertain when Sisko et al. are located, members of the *Defiant* crew randomly transport into Earth's past. They conclude Sisko et al. "arrived before the year twenty-forty-eight."

Odo: How can you be sure?

> **O'Brien**: Because we were just there. And that wasn't the mid-twenty-first century that I read about in school. It's been changed. *Earth history had its rough patches, but never that rough.*

Therefore, the absence of the Bell Uprising to spark the revolution that would politically challenge the current neoliberalism regime would ostensibly result in Earth's society devolving into some type of nightmare scenario as early as 2048.

The original timeline is restored when Sisko takes the name Gabriel Bell, and fulfills his role in history. One of the successes of the Bell Uprising was the ability of residents of the Sanctuary District to evade a government blockade of the "Interface" (i.e., the internet—which was a nascent technology when "Past Tense" aired in 1995) and convey their personal stories to the world. One resident explains: "My name is Henry Garcia . . . and I've been living here two years now. . . . I've never been in trouble with the law or anything. . . . I don't want to hurt anybody. . . . I just want a chance to work and live like regular people."

Confirming the interpretation of *Star Trek* as positing American history as a series of progressive events ("revolutions") is "The Savage Curtain" (1969—original series) and "The Omega Glory" (1968—original series). The episode "The Omega Glory" depicts a world with an identical history to that of Earth's, except in this instance the Cold War resulted in globally devastating nuclear/biological war—where humans were reduced to a veritable stone age. Kirk ultimately realizes that the segment of the population that represented the West views the U.S. Constitution as a sacred document. But they cannot read it, so Kirk explains to them: "That which you called Ee'd Plebnista was not written for chiefs or kings or warriors or the rich and powerful, but for all the people!" Kirk proceeds to read directly from this document (the Ee'd Plebnista), which is the Constitution:

> We the people of the United States, in order to form a more perfect union, establish justice, ensure domestic tranquility, provide for the common defense, promote the general welfare, and secure the blessings of liberty to ourselves and our posterity . . . do ordain and establish this constitution.

Asserting the revolutionary implications of the American Revolution and the Constitution that followed, Kirk declares "these words and the words that follow. . . . They must apply to everyone or they mean nothing!" Kirk adds "liberty and freedom have to be more than just words."

In "The Savage Curtain" the *Enterprise* crew meets the incarnation of Abraham Lincoln. While acknowledging that this is not the real Lincoln, Kirk insists that the crew treat him with the respect and deference due this great historical figure—the leader of what many consider to be the second American Revolution (i.e., the victorious Northern Cause in the

U.S. Civil War).[44] Kirk notes: "I cannot conceive it possible that Abraham Lincoln . . . could have actually been reincarnated. And yet his kindness, his gentle wisdom, his humor, everything about him is so right." McCoy chides Kirk: "Practically the entire crew has seen you . . . treat this impostor like the real thing . . . when he can't possibly be the real article. Lincoln died three centuries ago hundreds of light-years away." Spock observes to Kirk: "President Lincoln has always been a very personal hero to you." Kirk retorts: "Not only to me." Spock: "Agreed."

Thus, *Star Trek* is optimistic in that America is evolving toward an ideal, classless society. The American Revolution; the Civil War; the Bell Uprising (i.e., the defeat of neoliberalism) are necessary stops on this road to (worldwide) utopia. This is reflective of American Marxists' view that United States's history is an unfolding revolutionary process, the end result of which is the establishment of an ideal socialist/communist society. Sidney Hook, for instance, writing in 1933 (when he was still a Trotskyist) reasoned that "America had gone through her second revolution to break up the semi-feudal slavocracy which barred the expansion of industrial capitalism."[45] Operating in the United States since the 1920s, Trotskyists hold that the American Revolution and the Civil War remain incomplete until the worker state is in place. Put differently, these revolutions will be completed by the socialist revolution (the Bell Uprising[?]). (It is noteworthy and significant that in the episode where the Bell Uprising is conveyed, the phrase "Neo-Trotskyists" is used; also, in another episode, a passage from the Communist Manifesto is read.[46])

CONCLUSION

Within the context of the McCarthyism, analytic philosophy became dominant in American academia, as did (what can be labeled) an iterative-centered political science. In embracing analytic philosophy U.S. academicians turned away from justice—as engaging justice (academically) was deemed politically dangerous. The rejection of the philosophical treatment of justice has resulted in cynicism and enervation—with the nadir of the field manifest in the position of *intersubjective agreement* (where philosophy declares itself agnostic to the content of the politics, values of society). Alex Rosenberg, with his most recent book, takes this position further by holding justice claims (which are almost always informed by history) are (across the board) empirically wrong and catastrophically bad for society. Rosenberg is literally seeking to intellectually disarm the public by holding that the desire for justice, fairness is fundamentally irrational and always destructive. This would leave the field of politics to the forces of reaction, ignorance (*bullshit*), and repression.

I have countered the argumentation of analytic philosophy with that of Hegel and Marx—the idea of the progressive dialectic (illustrated, depicted through the *Star Trek* franchise [seemingly the most popular artistic vehicle in modern history]). Arguably, it is history as a progressive dialectic that is Rosenberg's target. The destruction of the progressive dialectic was the ideological aim of the Nazis.

NOTES

1. Donald Phillip Verene, *Hegel's Absolute: An Introduction to Reading the Phenomenology of Spirit* (Albany: State University New York Press, 2007); Stephen Houlgate, *Hegel's "Phenomenology of Spirit": A Reader's Guide* (New York: Bloomsbury Academic, 2013); Brady Bowman, *Hegel and the Metaphysics of Absolute Negativity* (Cambridge: Cambridge University Press, 2015).

2. Peter Singer, *Marx: A Very Short Introduction* (New York: Oxford University Press, 2001); Gareth Stedman Jones, *Karl Marx: Greatness and Illusion* (Cambridge: Cambridge University Press, 2016); Tom Rockmore, *Marx's Dream: From Capitalism to Communism* (Chicago: University of Chicago Press, 2018).

3. James P. Cannon, *The History of American Trotskyism: Report of a Participant* (New York: Pioneer Publishers, 1944); Constance Ashton Myers, *The Prophet's Army: Trotskyists in America, 1928–1941* (Westport, CT: Greenwood Press, 1977); A. Belden Fields, *Trotskyism and Maoism: Theory and Practice in France and the United States* (New York: Praeger, 1988), chap. 4; Bryan D. Palmer, *James P. Cannon and the Origins of the American Revolutionary Left, 1890–1928* (Urbana: University of Illinois Press, 2010); Donna T. Haverty-Stacke, *Trotskyists on Trial: Free Speech and Political Persecution since the Age of FDR* (New York: New York University Press, 2016).

4. Nicholas Capaldi, *The Enlightenment Project in the Analytic Conversation* (Boston: Kluwer Academic Publishers, 1998).

5. Hans-Johann Glock, *What Is Analytic Philosophy?* (New York: Cambridge University Press, 2008); Stephen P. Schwartz, *A Brief History of Analytic Philosophy: From Russell to Rawls* (West Sussex, UK: Wiley-Blackwell, 2012).

6. John McCumber, *Time in the Ditch: American Philosophy and the McCarthy Era* (Evansville: Northwestern University Press, 2001), and *The Philosophy Scare: The Politics of Reason in the Early Cold War* (Chicago: University of Chicago Press, 2016).

7. Daniel Little, *New Directions in the Philosophy of Social Science* (Lanham, MD: Rowman & Littlefield, 2016); Michael C. Desch, *Cult of the Irrelevant: The Waning Influence of Social Science on National Security* (Princeton: Princeton University Press, 2019), and "How Political Science Became Irrelevant," *Chronicle of Higher Education*, February 27, 2019. Web.

8. Yascha Mounk, "How Political Science Gets Politics Wrong," *Chronicle of Higher Education*, October 30, 2016. Web; Lee McIntyre, *Post-Truth* (Cambridge, MA: MIT Press, 2018).

9. Harold D. Lasswell, *Politics: Who Gets What, When, How* (New York: McGraw-Hill, 1936).

10. Donald Green and Ian Shapiro, *Pathologies of Rational Choice Theory: A Critique of Applications in Political Science* (New Haven: Yale University Press, 1996); Michael Allingham, *Choice Theory: A Very Short Introduction* (New York: Oxford University Press, 2002); Lina Eriksson, *Rational Choice Theory: Potential and Limits* (New York: Palgrave Macmillian, 2011).

11. John Rawls, *A Theory of Justice* (Cambridge, MA: Belknap, 1971).

12. Richard Rorty, *Philosophy and the Mirror of Nature* (Princeton: Princeton University Press, 1981); Michael Bacon, *Richard Rorty: Pragmatism and Political Liberalism* (Lanham: Lexington Books, 2007); Neil Gross, *Richard Rorty: The Making of an American Philosopher* (Chicago: University of Chicago Press, 2008).

In fairness, perhaps the most demoralized, deflating philosophical position is to acquiesce to the extinction of humanity vis-à-vis global warming. As philosophy professor Todd May does so in a *New York Times* op-ed piece, "Would Human Extinction Be a Tragedy?" *New York Times*, December 17, 2018. Web.

13. Alex Rosenberg, *How History Gets Things Wrong* (Cambridge, MA: MIT Press, 2018), 5.

14. Ibid.

15. Ibid., 6.

16. This is the title of a Nazi propaganda film, trumpeting the putative unity of the German people behind the Hitler regime.

17. Jane Caplan, *Nazi Germany (Short Oxford History of Germany)* (New York: Oxford University Press, 2008); Ian Kershaw, *Hitler, the Germans, and the Final Solution* (New Haven: Yale University Press, 2009), and *Hitler: A Biography* (New York: Norton, 2010).

18. George A. Gonzalez, *The Absolute and* Star Trek (New York: Palgrave Macmillan, 2017), 34.

19. George A. Gonzalez, *The Politics of* Star Trek: *Justice, War, and the Future* (New York: Palgrave Macmillan, 2015), and Star Trek *and the Politics of Globalism* (New York: Palgrave Macmillan, 2018).

20. Harry G. Frankfurt, *On Bullshit* (Princeton: Princeton University Press, 2005).

21. Rosenberg, *How History Gets Things Wrong*, 5.

22. Ibid., 6.

23. Frederick W. Meyer, *Narrative Politics: Stories and Collective Action* (New York: Oxford University Press, 2014); Jill Lepore, "Don't Let Nationalists Speak for the Nation," *New York Times*, May 26, 2019, SR3.

24. Steven Klein, "The New Science Wars: Radical Differences in the Humanities and Sciences Haven't Gone Away—They've Intensified," *Chronicle of Higher Education*, December 16, 2018. Web.

25. Roland Vegso, *The Naked Communist: Cold War Modernism and the Politics of Popular Culture* (New York: Fordham University Press, 2013). Modernism is a set of normative values that privileges reason and secularism, as opposed to obscurantism and political religion (i.e., theocracy). Peter Childs, *Modernism*, 3rd ed. (New York: Routledge, 2016).

26. Richard Carwardine and Jay Sexton, eds., *The Global Lincoln* (New York: Oxford University Press, 2011), ix

27. Sam Polk, a former hedge-fund trader, in a 2014 op-ed piece posited a critical assessment of the ethos that dominates the American finance community: "Wall Street is a toxic culture that encourages the grandiosity of people who are desperately trying to feel powerful." Sam Polk, "For the Love of Money," *New York Times*, January 19, 2014, SR1.

28. Karl Marx, *The Critique of the Gotha Programme* (London: Electric Book Co., 2001 [1875]), 20. Web.

29. *Deep Space Nine*—"Little Green Men," 1995.

30. Karl Marx, *On the Jewish Question*. 1844. Web.

31. Tom Rockmore, *Marx's Dream: From Capitalism to Communism* (Chicago: University of Chicago Press, 2018).

32. Marx, *The Critique of the Gotha Programme*, 20

33. http://www.st-minutiae.com/academy/literature329/457.txt.

34. Gérard Duménil and Dominique Lévy, *Capital Resurgent: Roots of the Neoliberal Revolution*, trans. Derek Jeffers (Cambridge, MA: Harvard University Press, 2004); Daniel Stedman Jones, *Masters of the Universe: Hayek, Friedman, and the Birth of Neoliberal Politics* (Princeton: Princeton University Press, 2012); Quinn Slobodian, *Globalists: The End of Empire and the Birth of Neoliberalism* (Cambridge, MA: Harvard University Press, 2018).

35. Guin A. McKee, *The Problem of Jobs: Liberalism, Race, and Deindustrialization in Philadelphia* (Chicago: University of Chicago Press, 2009); Timothy Williams, "For Shrinking Cities, Destruction Is a Path to Renewal," *New York Times*, November 12, 2013, A15.

36. Thomas J. Sugrue, *The Origins of the Urban Crisis: Race and Inequality in Postwar Detroit* (Princeton: Princeton University Press, 2005); Joe Drape,"Bankruptcy for Ailing Detroit, but Prosperity for Its Teams," *New York Times*, October 14, 2013, A1.

37. Carol Poh Miller and Robert Wheeler, *Cleveland: A Concise History* (Bloomington: Indiana University Press, 2009).

38. Mary Elizabeth Gallagher, *Contagious Capitalism: Globalization and the Politics of Labor in China* (Princeton: Princeton University Press, 2005); Kelly Sims Gallagher, *China Shifts Gears: Automakers, Oil, Pollution, and Development* (Cambridge, MA: MIT Press, 2006); Louis Uchitelle, "Goodbye, Production (and Maybe Innovation)." *New York Times*, December 24, 2006, sec. 3 p. 4; Peter S. Goodman, "U.S. and Global Economies Slipping in Unison," *New York Times*, August 24, 2008, A1; David Koistinen, *Confronting Decline: The Political Economy of Deindustrialization in Twentieth-Century New England* (Gainesville: University Press of Florida, 2013).

39. Susan M. Wachter and Kimberly A. Zeuli, eds., *Revitalizing American Cities* (Philadelphia: University of Pennsylvania Press, 2013); Monica Davey, "A Picture of Detroit Ruin, Street by Forlorn Street," *New York Times*, February 18, 2014, A1; Jon Hurdle, "Philadelphia Forges Plan to Rebuild From Decay," *New York Times*, January 1, 2014, B1.

40. Deborah K. Padgett, Benjamin F. Henwood, and Sam J. Tsemberis, *Housing First: Ending Homelessness, Transforming Systems, and Changing Lives* (New York: Oxford University Press, 2015); Craig Willse, *The Value of Homelessness: Managing Surplus Life in the United States* (Minneapolis: University of Minnesota Press, 2015).

41. Kristin S. Seefedt and John D. Graham, *America's Poor and the Great Recession* (Bloomington: Indiana University Press, 2013); "Ten States Still Have Fewer Jobs since Recession," *Reuters*, March 25, 2016; David Leonhardt, "We're Measuring the Economy All Wrong," *New York Times*, September 14, 2018. Web; Sabrina Tavernise, "Where Jobs Vanished, 'Nobody Had Our Backs,'" *New York Times*, May 28, 2019, A1.

42. Claire Cain Miller, "Smarter Robots Move Deeper Into Workplace," *New York Times*, December 16, 2014, A1, and "What's Really Killing Jobs? It's Automation, Not China," *New York Times*, December 22, 2016, A3; Liz Alderman, "Humans Wanted, But Robots Work," *New York Times*, April 17, 2018, B1; Kevin Roose, "The Automation Agenda Hidden by the Davos Elite," *New York Times*, January 26, 2019, B1; Eduardo Porter, "Technology Splits Work Force: High Pay for a Few and Low Pay for the Rest," *New York Times*, February 5, 2019, A17.

43. Paul Krugman, "Robots and Robber Barons," *New York Times*, December 10, 2012, A27.

44. James M. McPherson, *Abraham Lincoln and the Second American Revolution* (New York: Oxford University Press, 1992); James Oakes, *Freedom National: The Destruction of Slavery in the United States* (New York: W.W. Norton & Company, 2012).

45. Sidney Hook, *Towards the Understanding of Karl Marx* (New York: John Day, 1933), 294–95.

46. In the midst of a labor strike (*Deep Space Nine*—"Bar Association" 1996), a character reads directly from the *Communist Manifesto*: "Workers of the world, unite. You have nothing to lose but your chains."

TWO

Modernity and the Trump Turn

In *The Politics of* Star Trek I argue that the *Star Trek* franchise (the broadcast iterations) is the quintessential text of the modern era.[1] In this chapter I modify this formulation somewhat and hold that the franchise is the quintessential text of modernity. The *Star Trek* text references the two philosophical turns at the center of modernity: 1) the stoic turn, and the 2) the Socratic turn. More than making artistic references to the philosophic turns that serve as the basis of modernity, *Star Trek* speculates about (depicts) potential future turns that could profoundly shape society in the context of modernity: 1) a Marxist turn, 2) a Schmittian turn, and 3) a Trumpian turn (referring to U.S. President Donald J. Trump). *Star Trek: Discovery* (the latest series in the franchise) is precisely about this last potential (racist, supremacist) turn (during its first season).

THE PHILOSOPHICAL UNDERPINNINGS MODERNITY

The Stoic Turn refers to the primacy of reason over emotion. The practical significance is it represents a rejection of superstition, the occult, the supernatural, and an embrace of empiricism.[2] The stoic turn in the world of *Star Trek* is fictionally salient with the Vulcans. Mr. Spock, a Vulcan and first officer of the *Enterprise* in the original series, notes that: "I prefer the concrete, the graspable, the provable" ("The Return of The Archons" 1967). According to the backstory of the Vulcans, they were an tensely emotional people and this resulted in continual violence ("All Our Yesterdays" 1969). The ancient teachings of Surak (à la Buddha or Jesus Christ[3]) brought about a planet-wide movement of stoicism ("Savage Curtain" 1969). Mr. Spock's favorite phrase is (other than "fascinating") "logical"—or conversely "illogical"—intuitively critiquing any supposition he deems outside of the empirical and/or reason. In the West, stoicism becomes particularly widespread with the establishment of Christianity as the official religion of the Roman Empire.[4]

The Socratic Turn specifically refers to Socrates of ancient Greece.[5] Socrates is most famous for challenging the pagan theology and theocracy of ancient Athens. For this, he is executed. Socrates's defiance is artistically depicted in the original series episode of "Who Mourns for Adonis" (1967). The crew of the *Enterprise* comes across the god Apollo, who (along with the other gods of ancient Greek mythology) fled Earth when he ceased to be worshiped. Apollo captures the *Enterprise* with the hope of reviving humans' reverence of him. Captain Kirk defiantly informs Apollo that humans have "out grown" their pagan beliefs (as well as superstitions) and now embrace monotheism—presumably a deist theology.[6] Kirk to Apollo: "Mankind has no need for gods. We find the one quite adequate."

While Socrates was a fourth-century BCE figure, the Socratic Turn is part of the European Enlightenment of the seventeenth and eighteenth centuries.[7] The Socratic Turn is specifically the demand that the state and politics reflect rationality.[8] This directly challenges the monarchical, aristocratic claim that a ruling caste has been ordained by God.[9] The Socratic Turn and the Enlightenment comes to a head with Thomas Paine's renowned pamphlet *Common Sense* (where he expressly mocks the idea of monarchy and aristocracy) and the American Revolution (1776–1783) that was in significant part precipitated by this pamphlet. The affirmative rationality of the American Revolution is found in the phrase that "all men are created equal."[10]

The Socratic Turn of the Enlightenment is in part portrayed in the original series episode "Omega Glory" (1968). It depicts a world with an identical history to that of Earth's, except in this instance the Cold War resulted in globally devastating nuclear/biological war—where humans were reduced to a veritable stone age. Kirk ultimately realizes that the segment of the population that represented the West views the U.S. Constitution as a sacred document. But they cannot read it, so Kirk explains to them that it represents the Enlightenment concept of equality before the law: "That which you called Ee'd Plebnista was not written for chiefs or kings or warriors or the rich and powerful, but for all the people!" Kirk proceeds to read directly from this document (the Ee'd Plebnista), which is the Constitution:

> We the people of the United States, in order to form a more perfect union, establish justice, ensure domestic tranquility, provide for the common defense, promote the general welfare, and secure the blessings of liberty to ourselves and our posterity . . . do ordain and establish this constitution.

Asserting the revolutionary implications of the American Revolution and the Constitution that followed, Kirk declares "these words and the words that follow. . . . They must apply to everyone or they mean nothing!" Kirk adds "liberty and freedom have to be more than just words."

The other significant aspect of the Enlightenment portrayed in the *Star Trek* text is the U.S. Civil War—which resulted in the abolition of slavery (thereby serving to make "all men are created equal" more of a reality).[11] In "The Savage Curtain" (1969) the *Enterprise* crew meets the incarnation of Abraham Lincoln. While acknowledging that this is not the real Lincoln, Kirk insists that the crew treat him with the respect and deference due this great historical figure—the leader of what many consider to be the second American Revolution (i.e., the victorious Northern Cause in the U.S. Civil War).[12] Kirk notes: "I cannot conceive it possible that Abraham Lincoln . . . could have actually been reincarnated. And yet his kindness, his gentle wisdom, his humor, everything about him is so right." McCoy chides Kirk: "Practically the entire crew has seen you . . . treat this impostor like the real thing . . . when he can't possibly be the real article. Lincoln died three centuries ago hundreds of light-years away." Spock observes to Kirk: "President Lincoln has always been a very personal hero to you." Kirk retorts: "Not only to me." Spock: "Agreed."

The *Star Trek* text does more than document, it artistically depicts the two philosophic turns central to modernity. The creators of *Star Trek* speculate as to future philosophic (modernist) turns. The United Federation of Planets (the interstellar political institution that humans lead) represents a Marxist turn—described in chapter 1 as the *progressive dialectic*. *Star Trek*, beginning with the 1996 movie, *First Contact*, speculates as to a Schmittian turn. The series *Enterprise* (2001–2005) explores the inherent pitfalls of relying on the "other" as the basis of political legitimacy—namely, that it inherently results in racism. With the most recent *Star Trek* series, *Discovery* (2017 to present) a polity dominated by racism, supremacist reasoning, and warmongering is conveyed. This can be deemed the Trumpian turn.

THE "FRIEND/FOE" DICHOTOMY

Carl Schmitt (1888–1985) is in the pantheon of neoconservative thinkers. Schmitt was an architect of the Nazi Germany legal regime and known as the "Crown Jurist" of the Nazis.[13] He was an ostensive mentor to Leo Strauss (1899–1973), who was a German Jew that emigrated to the United States in 1937 because of the Nazis. (Strauss, in particular, is considered to be a lodestone for American neoconservatives.[14]) Schmitt wrote *The Concept of the Political* in 1929, and Strauss a set of sympathetic "Notes" to Schmitt's book.[15] Schmitt provided a letter of recommendation for Strauss that facilitated Strauss's obtaining an academic position at the University of Chicago.[16]

Schmitt held that at the center of politics is the distinction "between friend and enemy."[17] Social and political cohesion is based on this friend/foe dichotomy. Reflective of Schmitt's "friend/enemy" reasoning, in *The Next Generation* episode "Face of the Enemy" (1993) the point is made that Romulans have an "absolute certainty about . . . who is a friend and who is an enemy." The main component of Hitler's and the Nazis' political/propaganda argumentation was directed at an imaginary coalition of Western bankers and Eastern communists conspiring against Germany. According to Nazi mythology (myopia) Jews were at the center of this worldwide anti-Germany coalition. In the face of this global conspiracy directed against Germany, the Hitler regime argued that the German people must be unified (i.e., no dissent whatsoever), and strike back (i.e., World War II).[18] In her synthesis of Strauss's writings, Shadia B. Drury renders the following observation: "Like Schmitt, Strauss believes that politics is first and foremost about the distinction between WE and THEY. Strauss thinks that a political order can be stable only if it is united by an external threat."[19]

The *Star Trek* movie *First Contact* (1996) is predicated on a WE/THEY distinction. The action of the movie takes place in the year 2063. The Borg go back in Earth's history to prevent humanity's first contact with the Vulcans. This initial exposure to an alien culture occurs because Zephran Cochrane conducts humanity's first successful warp drive experiment. ("Warp speed" represents a speed faster than light.) When the Vulcans detect Cochrance's ship achieving warp speed they decide to introduce themselves to earthlings—"first contact." In this iteration (*First Contact*) of *Star Trek*'s historiography of Earth in 2063 humanity is in what is referred to a "Second Dark Age."[20] What rallies humanity from its disarray is its contact with the Vulcans: *"It unites humanity in a way no one ever thought possible when they realize they're not alone in the universe."*

Therefore, the political foundation of humanity in the mid-twenty-first-century is the WE/THEY dichotomy—with the Vulcans serving as "They." "The political enemy is not necessarily morally evil." Instead, Schmitt held that the potential enemy "is merely the other, the stranger, and it is sufficient that according to his nature he is in a special intense way existentially something different and alien, so that in the extreme case conflicts with him are possible."[21]

In *Enterprise* conflict with the Vulcans does occur. "The Andorian Incident" (2001) concludes with the exposure of a Vulcan "spy station" by Captain Archer, which earns the ire of the Vulcans. The Vulcan ambassador to Earth complains that "the Andorians wouldn't have found the [spy] station if your people hadn't interfered." The *Enterprise* has "been in space for six months and they've already destabilized an entire sector" ("Shadows of P'Jem" 2002). "Fusion" (2002) involves a set of Vulcans, who contrary to Vulcan norms, embrace their emotions. ("I always knew there had to be more to life than just logic and reason.") One of these

Vulcans telepathically "rapes" T'Pol (a Vulcan and *Enterprise*'s first officer), and Captain Archer engages in an intense fist fight with the transgressor. "The Forge" (2004), "Awakening" (2004), and the "Kir'Shara" (2004) is a three episode story arc whereby Earth's embassy on Vulcan is bombed, killing Admiral Forrest (Archer's mentor), and the *Enterprise* crew gets swept up in internal Vulcan religious and political strife—with an effort made against Captain Archer's life; and the *Enterprise* and Vulcan military ships coming to a face-off. In the denouement we learn that elements within the Vulcan government were behind the bombing of the Earth embassy, and that a faction still in the government wants to pull the planet toward a political/military alliance with the Romulans. An intention ominously threatening to Earth.

TERRA PRIME

The *Enterprise* series concludes in 2005 and the penultimate episode "Terra Prime" centers on the group Terra Prime. Initially, this organization is described as xenophobic: "They want to stop all contact with alien species." "They believe it's corrupting our way of life." Later, we learn that Terra Prime is racist: "This is an alien-human hybrid. Living proof of what will happen if we allow ourselves to be submerged in an interstellar coalition. Our genetic heritage. . . ." "That child is a cross-breed freak. How many generations before our genome is so diluted that the word human is nothing more than a footnote in some medical text?" The leader of Terra Prime declares "I'm returning Earth to its rightful owners." The group seeks to scuttle the formation of the Federation by promising to destroy Starfleet command (in San Francisco) unless all aliens leave Earth. Referring to signs of popular support for Terra Prime and its agenda, the Vulcan Ambassador Soval notes: "The fact that Paxton has the support of so many of your people is . . . troubling." An Andorian ambassador makes the point that: "Earthmen talk about uniting worlds, but your own planet is deeply divided. Perhaps you're not quite ready to host this conference" promoting interstellar cooperation.

While the creators of *Enterprise* indicate that a reliance on the "other" to maintain political stability and legitimacy could result in broad-based racism, the presidential administration of Donald J. Trump is directly predicated on racism, xenophobia, and even white supremacy. A polity based directly on these values is depicted in season 1 of the latest *Star Trek* series—*Discovery*.

A RACIST TURN?

U.S. President Donald J. Trump has based his government on expressly racist policies and rhetoric. His administration instituted a racist immigration policy of refusing entry to the United States of all citizens from a number of Islamic-majority countries.[22] Trump, himself, has issued blanket vilifications of undocumented immigrants (especially from Latin America)—casting them as criminal elements ("rapists," "animals") and an inherent threat to public safety.[23] Perhaps most egregious of all, President Trump offered political support to white supremacist groups and their violence when he refused to condemn the fact that one of their members wantonly murdered a counterprotester during a 2017 protest in Charlottesville, Virginia. In direct response to the fact that a white supremacist knowingly drove his automobile into a crowd and killed someone, Trump speciously held "I think there is blame on both sides."[24]

In the *Star Trek* series *Discovery* the Klingons represent a racist, supremacist entity. Mirroring the "Unite the Right" campaign of white supremacist groups,[25] the goal of the leading Klingon (T'Kuvma) at the beginning of the series is to unite the different factions ("houses") of Klingon society for a war against the Federation. This leader is expressly racist, xenophobic, and supremacist ("Vulcan Hello" 2017). T'Kuvma:

> They are coming . . . atom by atom . . . they will coil around us . . . and take all that we are. There is one way to confront this threat. By reuniting the twenty-four warring houses of our own empire.
>
> Together under one creed . . . Remain Klingon! . . . To lock arms against those whose fatal greeting is . . . WE COME IN PEACE!
>
> Our Purity is a threat to them. They wish to drag us into the muck where humans, Vulcans, Tellerites, and fifthy Andorians mix.

Importantly, when first contact is made with the Klingons, Michael Burnham, the lead character of the series, argues that firing on the Klingons (a "Vulcan Hello"—episode title) is the only way to establish stable relations with them—"Violence brought respect." Later, the Klingons are conveyed as monstrous—as they eat a human body. The insinuation is white supremacists (who are solely motivated by hate, racism, xenophobia) are not to be reasoned with. Indeed, they are outside of reason.

This is a decidedly different tack than the one recently pursued by the *New York Times*, which did a "soft" (or human interest) article on a white supremacist and his white supremacist wife.[26] Even more recently, the *New York Times* bolstered the bigoted (and paranoid) views of a losing candidate for the Pennsylvania state legislature. The candidate and a clutch of his supporters (after conceding defeat and imbibing pitchers of beer) communicated during the election night party "a conscious fear around what they see as the replacement of traditional, white American culture" and the "belief that the country is being undermined by undeserving outsiders." Despite the fact that this candidate had lost by a wide margin, the writer for the *Times* avers (without any empirical evidence whatsoever) that a "shift" in "the political winds" toward hate and bigotry "is growing stronger."[27]

CONCLUSION

The *Star Trek* text references the two philosophical turns at the center of modernity: 1) the stoic turn, and the 2) the Socratic turn. More than making artistic references to the philosophic turns that serve as the basis of modernity, *Star Trek* speculates about (depicts) potential future turns that could profoundly shape society in the context of modernity: 1) a Marxist turn, 2) a Schmittian turn, and 3) a Trumpian turn (referring to U.S. President Donald J. Trump). The *Star Trek* text issues strong warnings against the latter two turns. Indeed, the Schmittian and Trumpian turns can be viewed as a single piece: the politics of the "other" leads directly to a political regime of racism and supremacist reasoning. Therefore, it would appear that (according the *Star Trek* text) the Marxist turn is the only future where humanity, fairness, and justice thrives.

NOTES

1. George A. Gonzalez, *The Politics of* Star Trek*: Justice, War, and the Future* (New York: Palgrave Macmillan, 2015), and *The Absolute and* Star Trek (New York: Palgrave Macmillan, 2017).
2. John Sellars, *Stoicism* (Los Angeles: University of California Press, 2006).
3. Michael D. Coogan, ed., *Eastern Religions: Hinduism, Buddism, Taoism, Confucianism, Shinto* (New York: Oxford University Press, 2005); Willard G. Oxtoby, Roy C. Amore, and Amir Hussain, *World Religions: Eastern Traditions*, 4th ed. (New York: Oxford University Press, 2014); C. Kavin Rowe, *One True Life: The Stoics and Early Christians as Rival Traditions* (New Haven: Yale University Press, 2016).
4. Runar Thorsteinsson, *Roman Christianity and Roman Stoicism: A Comparative Study of Ancient Morality* (New York: Oxford University Press, 2013).
5. Paul Johnson, *Socrates: A Man for Our Times* (New York: Penguin, 2012).
6. Jeffrey R. Wigelsworth, *Deism in Enlightment England: Theology, Politics, and Newtonian Public Science* (Manchester: Manchester University Press, 2009).
7. Michael Trapp, ed., *Socrates from Antiquity to the Enlightenment* (New York: Routledge, 2007); Dorinda Outram, *The Enlightenment*, 3rd ed. (New York: Cambridge University Press, 2013).
8. Dustin Sebell, *The Socratic Turn: Knowledge of Good and Evil in an Age of Science* (Philadelphia: University of Pennsylvania Press, 2016).
9. Jonathan I. Israel, *Radical Enlightenment: Philosophy and the Making of Modernity, 1650–1750* (New York: Oxford University Press, 2001), and *Enlightenment Contested: Philosophy, Modernity, and the Emancipation of Man, 1670–1752* (New York: Oxford University Press, 2006).
10. Craig Nelson, *Thomas Paine: Enlightenment, Revolution, and the Birth of Modern Nations* (New York: Penguin, 2007); Joseph F. Kett, *Merit: The History of a Founding Ideal From the American Revolution to the Twenty-First Century* (Ithaca, NY: Cornell University Press, 2013); Jonathan I. Israel, *The Expanding Blaze: How the American Revolution Ignited the World, 1775–1848* (Princeton: Princeton University Press, 2017).
11. Elizabeth R. Varon, *Disunion!: The Coming of the American Civil War, 1789–1859* (Chapel Hill: University of North Carolina Press, 2010).

12. James M. McPherson, *Abraham Lincoln and the Second American Revolution* (New York: Oxford University Press, 1992); James Oakes, *Freedom National: The Destruction of Slavery in the United States* (New York: W.W. Norton & Company, 2012).

13. Joseph W. Bendersky, *Carl Schmitt: Theorist for the Reich* (Princeton, NJ: Princeton University Press, 1983).

14. Anne Norton, *Leo Strauss and the Politics of American Empire* (New Haven: Yale University Press, 2004); Francis Fukuyama, "After Neoconservatism," *New York Times Magazine*, February 19, 2006, 62.

15. Leo Strauss,"Notes on Carl Schmitt, *The Concept of the Political*," in *The Concept of the Political*, expanded edition, by Carl Schmitt (Chicago: University of Chicago Press, 2007 [1932]).

16. Daniel Tanguay, *Leo Strauss: An Intellectual Biography* (New Haven: Yale University Press, 2007); Steven B. Smith, "Leo Strauss: The Outlines of a Life," in *Cambridge Companion to Leo Strauss*, ed. Steven B. Smith (New York: Cambridge University Press, 2009), 18.

17. "The specific political distinction to which political actions and motives can be reduced is that between friend and enemy." Carl Schmitt, *The Concept of the Political*, expanded edition (Chicago: University of Chicago University, 2007 [1929]), 26.

18. Jane Caplan, *Nazi Germany* (New York: Oxford University Press, 2008); Jeffrey Herf, *The Jewish Enemy: Nazi Propaganda during World War II and the Holocaust* (Cambridge, MA: Harvard University Press, 2008).

19. Shadia B. Drury, *Leo Strauss and the American Right* (New York: St. Martin's Press, 1997), 23.

20. The script notes to the movie: "A Third World War. Nuclear explosions, environmental disasters, tens of millions dead. The United States ceases to exist. All political authority vanishes. Humanity teetering on the edge of the Second Dark Age." http://www.st-minutiae.com/academy/literature329/fc.txt

21. Schmitt, *The Concept of the Political*, 27.

22. Michael D. Shear, "Trump Imposes New Travel Ban on 7 Countries," *New York Times*, September 25, 2017, A1.

23. Alexander Burns, "Pushing Someone Rich, Trump Offers Himself," *New York Times*, June 17, 2015, A16; also see David Leonhardt, "Trump Encourages Violence," *New York Times*, March 18, 2019, A23.

24. Michael D. Shear and Maggie Haberman, "Trump Again Says Two Sides at Fault in Rally Violence," *New York Times*, August 16, 2017, A1.

25. Sheryl Gay Stolberg and Brian M. Rosenthal, "White Nationalist Protest Leads to Deadly Violence," *New York Times*, August 13, 2017, A1.

26. Richard Fausset, "In America's Heartland, the Voice of Hate Next Door," *New York Times*, November 26, 2017, A16.

27. Astead W. Herndon, "'Witch Hunts' and 'Fake News': Trump Grievances Go Local," *New York Times*, March 17, 2019, A20.

THREE

Neoliberalist World System as Dystopia

What is dystopia? Two philosophical traditions can be used to answer this question: 1) pragmatism/neopragmatism; and 2) the Hegelian Absolute. For the pragmatism position, politics, ethics is about maintaining social stability. Therefore, social breakdown, the absence of state authority, anarchy—represents dystopia. For Georg Hegel, dystopia is the unjust society—i.e., a "bad infinity." Judging by the dysfunction of neoliberalist elites (e.g., Donald Trump), neoliberalism is a dystopia—i.e., a bad infinity. To compare the Hegelian Absolute and pragmatism/neopragmatism I rely on popular culture, and, especially the broadcast iterations of the *Star Trek* franchise. The science fiction genre is particularly noted for speculating about future society as dystopia.[1]

DYSTOPIA IN PRAGMATISM/NEOPRAGMATISM

When viewed through the prism of dystopia it becomes evident that what entrenched elites offer is stability, not justice. Harvard historian Louis Menand points out that the core of *pragmatism* is "the belief that ideas [ethics, morality] should never become ideologies"—which early pragmatists (William James and Charles Pierce most prominently) saw as the cause of the American Civil War.[2] Therefore, pragmatists seemingly hold that concepts of justice or political principles should not precede the goal of maintaining social stability.[3] To do so invites devastating conflict (e.g., the American Civil War) and chaos. It is political/societal stability, and not justice (per se), that allows for social, economic, and technological progress.[4]

Star Trek, in the original series episode "Bread and Circuses" (1968), is ostensibly critical of *pragmatism* and its overriding emphasis on societal stability—with the outcome being the persistence of slavery worldwide. The *Enterprise* crew comes upon a planet that is virtually identical to mid-twentieth-century Earth (America); except on this world the Roman Empire never collapsed and, instead, spans the entire planet. "A world ruled by emperors who can trace their line back 2,000 years to their own Julius and Augustus Caesars." The result is that slavery continues—in part because the slave system was reformed to maintain its stability: "Long ago, there were [slave] rebellions" but "with each century, the slaves acquired more rights under the law. They received rights to medicine, the right to government payments in their old age, and they slowly learned to be content." Spock: "Slavery evolving into an institution with guaranteed medical payments, old-age pensions." In defending this society, one of the characters explains: "This is an ordered world, a conservative world based on time-honored Roman strengths and virtues. . . . There's been no war here for over four hundred years." "Could your land of that same era make that same boast?," he asks of the *Enterprise* landing party (specifically Kirk and McCoy). Explaining why Federation citizens who had come upon this Rome-like world could not be allowed to leave (thereby having the opportunity to tell others of its existence): "I think you can see why they don't want to have their *stability* contaminated by dangerous ideas of other ways and places"—i.e., *ideologies* of freedom, democracy, equality, etc., that could be politically destabilizing. Spock, in response, opines: "given a conservative empire, quite understandable."

Another American philosopher, Richard Rorty, writing in the early 1980s, in fashioning *neopragmatism* argues that societies are based on *intersubjective agreement*.[5] Thus, what is required for societal stability is enough consensus on a set of ideas—any set of ideas. Hence, what matters is consensus, and not the ideas themselves. Presumably, when there is not enough intersubjective consensus/agreement, then social/political breakdown occurs.

Over ten years before Rorty published his path-breaking notion of *intersubjective agreement*, the *Star Trek*, original series (1966–1969), episode "Mirror, Mirror" (1967) aired. Members of the *Enterprise* crew (including Kirk and McCoy), through a technical glitch, are beamed to an alternate universe. The *Enterprise* (including Spock) exists in this alternate universe, but instead of the Federation the political authority is the "Empire"—where "behavior and discipline" is "brutal, savage." Captain Kirk (from the Federation) refuses to carry out the order to destroy a planet that refuses to comply with the Empire. Spock (sporting a mustache and goatee) notes to Kirk: "No one will question the assassination of a captain who has disobeyed prime orders of the Empire." Kirk: "I command an *Enterprise* where officers apparently employ private henchmen among the crew, where assassination of superiors is a common means of advancing in rank." McCoy asks, "What kind of people are we in this universe?":

Kirk: Let's find out.

Kirk (to the ship's computer): Read out official record of current command.

Computer: Captain James T. Kirk succeeded to command I.S.S. *Enterprise* through assassination of Captain Christopher Pike. First action—suppression of Gorlan uprising through destruction of rebel home planet. Second action—execution of five thousand colonists on Vega 9.

Kirk (interrupting the computer): Cancel.

McCoy: Now we know.

Captain Jonathan Archer (*Star Trek: Enterprise* [2001–2005]) from the alternative universe declares that "Great men are not peacemakers. Great men are conquerors" ("In a Mirror, Darkly" 2005). The implication of "Mirror, Mirror" (and "In a Mirror, Darkly") is irrespective of their value system—whether "Empire" or "Federation"—humans can create and lead a vast interstellar political formation. Technological progress and political stability would essentially be the same.

The *intersubjective agreement* argument in "Mirror, Mirror" is brought into sharper relief in *Deep Space Nine* (1993–1999) where the alternate universe is revisited a century later in the episode "Crossover" (1994). We learn that Kirk's time in the alternate universe had a profound impact. "On my side, Kirk is one of the most famous names in our history." In "Mirror, Mirror" Kirk apprised Spock of a weapon ("the Tantalus field"). From one's quarters a person could zero in on victims and with the push of a button make them disappear. Kirk counseled Spock to use such technology to profoundly change the Empire, and base it on the values of the Federation. When Spock, however, disrupts the *intersubjective agreement* that was the basis of the Empire it collapses:

> Almost a century ago, a Terran starship Captain named James Kirk accidentally exchanged places with his counterpart from your side due to a transporter accident. Our Terrans were barbarians then, but their Empire was strong. While your Kirk was on this side, he met a Vulcan named Spock and somehow had a profound influence on him. Afterwards, Spock rose to commander in chief of the Empire by preaching reforms, disarmament, peace. It was a remarkable turnabout for his people. Unfortunately for them, when Spock had completed all these reforms, his empire was no longer in any position to defend itself against us.

The end result is that the Earth is conquered and occupied—with Terrans as little more than slaves, whose lives have no value.

This serves as a parable for the pragmatist, neopragmatist—justice, fairness should never precede stability (even for a violent empire—e.g., the contemporary United States). Numerous American movies have posited the kind of dystopia outlined in "Crossover"—social breakdown, horribly unimaginable societal-wide oppression, population collapse, chaos, etc. Rather humorously, the *Simpsons* in a 2015 episode ("Let's Go Fly a Coot") takes note of this—with Homer using the length of a movie to list all the dystopian, apocalyptic films released of late:

> **Homer**: Ooh, previews!
>
> **Trailer Announcer**: In a dystopian future . . .
>
> **Homer**: Finally! A movie about a dystopian future, unlike *The Hunger Games, Edge of Tomorrow, Oblivion, Elysium, Snow Piercer, The Hunger Games: Catching Fire, X-Men: Days of Future Past, Ender's Game, The Road, World War Z, Children of Men, After Earth, I Am Legend, Mad Max: Fury Road, The Maze Runner, District Nine, The Purge, Looper, Cloud Atlas, Divergent, Insurgent, The Island* . . . [Homer keeps naming movies]
>
> **Movie Usher**: Sir, the movie's been over for 20 minutes. You'll have to clear out of the theater and come back for the next show.

This seeming surfeit of dystopian movies, mocked by the *Simpsons*, could be read two ways: first, the broad idea that society is currently losing stability—global warming, social decay (deindustrialization), a crisis of political legitimacy—and this portends profound social breakdown, chaos. Second, that unless people cling to the present (neoliberalist) social order violent anarchy will ensue. Therefore, such movies represent a threat or warning to the populace—if the status quo falters (however unpopular) the outcome will be a nightmare.

This elides the issue of whether the current neoliberalist world system is itself a dystopia.[6] This brings us to the Hegelian *absolute*. The argument is that justice exists as a metaphysic—as part of the absolute. The absolute is a fifth dimension where normative values inhere—fairness, red, hard, soft, *ad infinitum*. Thus, the Hegelian critic will argue that a society predicated on injustice is a dystopia—where unfairness reigns and people are unauthentic (i.e., living lives that lack fulfillment).[7] What are the telltale signs of a dystopia in the Hegelian vein?

Before I engage this question, I'll point out that the Hegelian argument brings into relief that pragmatism/neopragmatism lacks a specified notion of dystopia. The lack of stability is hardly a concrete definition for dystopia, and sometimes societal instability is desirable. Many/Most would want a Nazi-like regime/society to lack stability and pray for its collapse. Importantly, it's not clear at all that pragmatists, neopragmatists would celebrate the destabilizing of even a Nazi-dominated society. Put differently, there is nothing inherent to pragmatism/neopragmatism that would lead one to think that Nazism is a dystopia. With the American Donald J. Trump government embracing white supremacy,[8] this is not an idle issue. Similarly, the *New York Times* recently published an editorial that suggested that the extinction of humanity vis-à-vis global warming could be a good thing.[9] Hence, the *New York Times* prefers not to declare that the present society (on a direct course to self-destruction) is a dystopia.

In the end, pragmatism/neopragmatism may not be philosophies at all but only rank propaganda for whatever corrupt, destructive regime is of the moment. *The Man in the High Castle* (Amazon Prime) depicts a United States in the early 1960s that is conquered, occupied as a result World War Two. In Nazi/Japan occupied America viewers are shown political advertisements encouraging people to be pragmatic. They should focus on the fact that they have jobs and that they are contributing to a "strong" (i.e., stable) nation. *Star Trek*, the original series, in the 1960s linked pragmatism and Nazism. In "Patterns of Force" (1968) a renowned Federation historian is sent to a relatively primitive planet (Ekos) as a "cultural observer." Nevertheless, in an effort to stabilize the planet's society the historian models its politics on Nazi Germany. When the historian (named Gill) is asked why he interfered in the primitive planet's politics/social organization, he responds (in a drugged stupor): "Planet . . . fragmented . . . divided. Took lesson from Earth history." "Why Nazi Germany?" as a model. Gill: "You studied history. You knew what the Nazis were. Most efficient state . . . Earth ever knew."

Carl Schmitt added to pragmatism (i.e., theorizing about political stability) racialist reasoning, which was ultimately mirrored (perniciously) by the German Nazis. Schmitt, as noted above, held that at the center of politics is the distinction "between friend and enemy." Social and political cohesion/stability is based on this friend/foe dichotomy.

"Patterns of Force," as noted above, portrays a Nazi regime on the planet of Ekos—which was instituted/sponsored/overseen by a Federation official. With Nazism as the political basis of Ekos, the Ekosians organize around the vilification of Zeons—a population from the neighboring planet of Zeon. ("Why do the Nazis hate Zeons?" "*Because without us to hate, there'd be nothing to hold them together*. So the Party has built us into a threat, a disease to be wiped out.") In addition to massacring the Zeons on Ekos ("the eliminations have started. Within an hour, the Zeon blight will forever be removed from Ekos"), the Nazi regime organizes a planned genocide ("Their Final Solution") against Zeons on their home planet: "Our entire solar system will forever be rid of the disease that was Zeon."

While pragmatism/neopragmatism ostensibly embraces societal stability—above all other values—and fails to identify a dystopia in a useful manner, Hegelian reasoning does point to what a dystopia is. Hegel himself wrote of "bad infinities"—or societies at odds with values of the Absolute. Hence, for Hegel, societies could be stable and functional but its residents could be leading unfulfilling, inauthentic lives (i.e., a dystopia). Karl Marx specifies this reasoning in arguing that the ideal society was one that is modern, classless, and free of gender and ethnic biases. (Marx saw his own work as an extension, specification, and corrective to that of Hegel's.)[10] If this is the ideal society, then every society that lacks all these characteristics can be viewed as a dystopia. Following from this, people in these societies are leading inauthentic, unfulfilling lives. Indeed, this thinking is at the core of Marx's entire theoretical edifice.[11] While Marx focused on the economic, material relations of societies to explain progressive revolutions, it is still the case that people in non-ideal societies (dystopias) feel unfulfilled, unauthentic, or "alienated."[12] This is arguably the prime normative factor propelling the forward movement of society toward the ideal—modern, classless, and free of gender and ethnic biases.

This still leaves us with the question: What are the telltale signs of a dystopia in the Hegelian (Marxian) vein? One indicator is dysfunctional elites.

DYSTOPIA IN THE HEGELIAN ABSOLUTE

Presumably, in a class unequal society the elites would be happy, content, and the most advanced members. After all the social structure is skewed to disproportionately, predominately benefit them (wealth, leisure time, education). Therefore, if the elites are somehow dysfunctional, it points to something being profoundly wrong with this society. As part of his indictment of capitalist society, Marx holds that its elites are boorish: "Contempt for theory, art, history, and for man as an end in himself . . . is the real, conscious standpoint, the virtue of the man of money."[13] The American president and longtime billionaire Donald J. Trump typifies the uncouth, anti-intellectual, even profane capitalist Marx identified over a century ago. Trump doesn't read, and denies global warming.[14] He's a misogynist,[15] employs vulgar, coarse language in describing others,[16] and has openly associated himself with the pornography industry.[17]

The documentary *Born Rich* (2003) indicates that the scions of the extremely wealthy suffer from severe ennui—indicating that a (neoliberalist) global society geared almost exclusively toward capital accumulation is misguided.[18] The unhappiness of capitalist elites is at the center of the television series *Mad Men* (2007–2015). Don Draper, the lead character, is at the top of the advertising industry during the Golden Age of the American economy—the 1950s into the mid-1960s. Draper philanders, smokes, and drinks heavily to cope with the seeming emptiness of his life—ultimately leaving the business world and his wealth to join a commune.

More broadly, Sam Polk, a former Wall Street trader, in 2014 published an op-ed piece in the *New York Times* where he argues *wealth addiction*[19] is rampant among the upper echelon of the American financial community.[20] Prior to coming to Wall Street Polk was a recovering drug addict. This experience as a drug addict, he argues, allowed him to see and diagnosis himself and others as literally addicted to wealth. Polk describes that even as he was making millions he "was a giant fireball of greed." "I wanted a billion dollars. It's staggering to think that in the course of five years, I'd gone from being thrilled at my first bonus—$40,000—to being disappointed when, my second year at the hedge fund, I was paid 'only' $1.5 million." Polk explains that "in the end, it was actually my absurdly wealthy bosses who helped me see the limitations of unlimited wealth." Polk was taken aback by their hostility to any effort to limit their amassing of wealth—even if such efforts could strengthen the financial system. (Polk quotes one of his unnamed superiors as stating: "I don't have the brain capacity to think about the system as a whole. All I'm concerned with is how this affects our company.") Polk concludes that his boss "was afraid of losing money, despite all that he had" and begins to determine that such fears were rooted in addiction:

> From that moment on, I started to see Wall Street with new eyes. I noticed the vitriol that traders directed at the government for limiting bonuses after the crash [of 2008]. I heard the fury in their voices at the mention of higher taxes. These traders despised anything or anyone that threatened their bonuses. Ever see what a drug addict is like when he's used up his junk? He'll do anything—walk twenty miles in the snow, rob a grandma—to get a fix. Wall Street was like that.

Polk holds that upon leaving Wall Street he suffered "withdrawal" symptoms.

THE DYSFUNCTION OF CAPITALIST ELITES LEADING TO (NEOLIBERALIST) DYSTOPIA

Polk argues that just like the addict is indifferent, blind to the pain and suffering he causes in feeding his addiction, much of America's economic elite is similarly unconcerned by the social and economic distress being caused by the operation of neoliberal capitalism (the unregulated movement of capital worldwide):

> Only a wealth addict would feel justified in receiving $14 million in compensation—including an $8.5 million bonus—as the McDonald's C.E.O., Don Thompson, did in 2012, while his company then published a brochure for its work force on how to survive on their low wages. Only a wealth addict would earn hundreds of millions as a hedge-fund manager, and then lobby to maintain a tax loophole that gave him a lower tax rate than his secretary.

Indifference to the social effects of a profit-making regime is conveyed in the *Star Trek: Voyager* episode "False Profits" (1996). A pair of Ferengi (Arridor and Kol) manipulate a planet's religious beliefs to install themselves as its leaders. Before the arrival of the Ferengis the native population (we are told) was "flourishing." Under the Ferengis profit-making regime the Ferengi become very wealthy, and at the same time poverty proliferates among the native population. ("The two Ferengi live in a palatial temple, while the people are lucky to have a roof over their heads.") Arridor and Kol are completely inured to the suffering they've caused, only celebrating the wealth they've accumulated. As noted above, the *Star Trek: Deep Space Nine* episode "Past Tense" (1995) depicts the social misery seemingly caused by global neoliberalism.

Another case of wealth addiction is portrayed in *Star Trek: The Next Generation* episode "The Neutral Zone" (1988). A capitalist, Ralph Offenhouse, from the late twentieth century is awoken from a cryogenic sleep. Immediately, Offenhouse's mind turns to his money: "I have a substantial portfolio. It's critical I check on it." Later, he adds "I have to phone Geneva right away about my accounts. The interest alone could be enough to buy even this ship." Subsequently, Captain Picard informs Ralph that "a lot has changed in three hundred years. People are no longer obsessed with the accumulation of 'things.' We have eliminated hunger, want, the need for possessions. We have grown out of our infancy." Ralph: "You've got it wrong. It's never been about 'possessions'—it's about power." Significantly, Polk in his op-ed piece holds that "Wall Street is a toxic culture that encourages the grandiosity of people who are desperately trying to feel powerful." Picard asks Ralph: "Power to do what?"

> **Ralph**: To control your life, your destiny.
>
> **Picard**: That kind of control is an illusion.

This notion of *controlling your life, your destiny* is particularly illusory in a context where the planet is warming dangerously and the biosphere is becoming destabilized as a result. Saliently, the wealth accumulation process is at the core of this planetary warming, destabilization.[21] Again, like drug addicts, wealth addicts are inured to the immense damage that their addiction causes others and themselves. The *Voyager* episode "Future's

End" (1996) features a technology capitalist (Ed Starling) who in 1996 threatens to destroy Los Angeles and is mute to the fact that his effort to travel into the future to bolster the fortunes of his corporation will destroy the solar system in the twenty-ninth century.

Therefore, *Star Trek* indicates that unbridled greed is pernicious, and can result in wealth addiction—as indicated with the Ferengi (who elevate profit making to a religion)[22] and Ralph Offenhouse (who obsesses about his financial holdings). Moreover, a society predicated on neoliberalism and the unrelenting pursuit of wealth, profit results in widespread social misery (dystopia), as conveyed in the episodes "False Profits" and "Past Tense."

CONCLUSION

What is a dystopia? Both pragmatism/neopragmatism and Hegelian philosophizing proffer answers as to what a dystopia is. At the core of pragmatism is a clear bifurcation or binary—either a society is stable or a dystopia. This makes pragmatism the philosophy of the status quo—for with the end or collapse of the regime/society of the moment a terrible chaos will ensue (e.g., the American Civil War). While this might make for interesting (or terrifying) science fiction movies and the like, it does not rise to an actual philosophical position—as pragmatists don't explain why stability is always preferable to social breakdown. The collapse of the Southern slavocracy was undoubtedly a good thing for the slaves that were freed as a result. A similar point can be made about the collapse of the Hitler regime and the groups targeted for elimination by it.

Hegelian reasoning about the Absolute brings us closer to philosophically identifying a society that is a dystopia. Social and political progress is about changing dystopias and moving them toward ideal societies. Marx, drawing on Hegel, holds that the ideal society is one that is modern, classless, and free of gender and ethnic biases. Revolutions on the path toward this ideal society are motivated by the inauthentic, alienation that the mass public feels in dystopias that are marked by wealth addiction among hegemonic elites and the poverty, social decay, and environmental destruction that results.

NOTES

1. Lars Schmeink, *Biopunk Dystopias Genetic Engineering, Society and Science Fiction* (Liverpool: Liverpool University Press, 2017); Adam Stock, *Modern Dystopian Fiction and Political Thought* (New York: Routledge, 2019).

2. Louis Menand, *The Metaphysical Club* (New York: Farrar, Straus, and Giroux, 2001), xii; also see Frank X. Ryan, Brian E. Butler, and James A. Good, eds. *The Real Metaphysical Club* (Albany: State University of New York Press, 2019).

3. Robert Danisch, *Pragmatism, Democracy, and the Necessity of Rhetoric* (Columbia: University of South Carolina Press, 2007); Larry A. Hickman, *Pragmatism as Post-Modernism: Lessons from John Dewey* (New York: Fordham University Press, 2007); Alan Malachowski, *The New Pragmatism* (Montreal: McGill-Queen's University Press, 2010); Michael Bacon, *Pragmatism* (Cambridge: Polity, 2012); Cheryl Misak, *The American Pragmatists* (New York: Oxford University Press, 2015).

4. Richard Tuck, *Hobbes: A Very Short Introduction* (New York: Oxford University Press, 2002); Noel Malcolm, ed., *Thomas Hobbes: Leviathan* (New York: Oxford University Press, 2012 [1668]).

5. Richard Rorty, *Philosophy and the Mirror of Nature* (Princeton: Princeton University Press, 1981); Michael Bacon, *Richard Rorty: Pragmatism and Political Liberalism* (Lanham: Lexington Books, 2007); Neil Gross, *Richard Rorty: The Making of an American Philosopher* (Chicago: University of Chicago Press, 2008).

6. Kate Brown, *Dispatches from Dystopia: Histories of Places Not Yet Forgotten* (Chicago: University of Chicago Press, 2015).

7. Donald Phillip Verene, *Hegel's Absolute: An Introduction to Reading the Phenomenology of Spirit* (Albany: State University New York Press, 2007); Stephen Houlgate, *Hegel's "Phenomenology of Spirit": A Reader's Guide* (New York: Bloomsbury Academic, 2013); Brady Bowman, *Hegel and the Metaphysics of Absolute Negativity* (Cambridge: Cambridge University Press, 2015); James Kreines, *Reason in the World: Hegel's Metaphysics and Its Philosophical Appeal* (New York: Oxford University Press, 2015); Andrew Feenberg, *Technosystem: The Social Life of Reason* (Cambridge, MA: Harvard University Press, 2017).

8. Michael D. Shear and Maggie Haberman, "Trump Again Says Two Sides at Fault in Rally Violence," *New York Times*, August 16, 2017, A1.

9. Todd May, "Would Human Extinction Be a Tragedy?" *New York Times*, December 17, 2018. Web.

10. Gareth Stedman Jones, *Karl Marx: Greatness and Illusion* (Cambridge: Cambridge University Press, 2016); Tom Rockmore, *Marx's Dream: From Capitalism to Communism* (Chicago: University of Chicago Press, 2018).

11. Peter Singer, *Marx: A Very Short Introduction* (New York: Oxford University Press, 2001).

12. Michael L. Schwalbe, *Psychosocial Consequences of Natural and Alienated Labor* (Albany: State University of New York Press, 1986).

13. Karl Marx, *On the Jewish Question*, 1844, http:// www.marxists.org/archive/ marx/ works/ 1844/jewish-question/.

14. Katie Rogers, "Books Trump Can Praise without Reading a Word," *New York Times*, December 1, 2018, A18; Coral Davenport and Mark Landler, "In Climate Fight, Trump Will Put Science on Trial," *New York Times*, May 28, 2019, A1.

15. Michael M. Grynbaum and John Koblin, "TV Host 'Ashamed' of Lewd Chat with Trump," *New York Times*, October 8, 2016, A12; "Transcript: Donald Trump's Taped Comments about Women," *New York Times*, October 8, 2016. Web; Billy Bush, "Yes, Donald Trump, You Said That," *New York Times*, December 4, 2017, A21.

16. Kimon de Greef and Sewell Chan, "Setback for U.S. Is Feared as Africa Recoils at Trump Remark," *New York Times*, January 16, 2018, A8.

17. David Moye, "Donald Trump Appeared In a Playboy Softcore Porn Video," *Huffington Post*, September 30, 2016. Web.

18. Daniel Stedman Jones, *Masters of the Universe: Hayek, Friedman, and the Birth of Neoliberal Politics* (Princeton: Princeton University Press, 2012); Adam Kotsko, *Neoliberalism's Demons: On the Political Theology of Late Capital* (Stanford: Stanford University Press, 2018).

19. Philip E. Slater, *Wealth Addiction* (New York: Dutton, 1980).

20. Sam Polk, "For the Love of Money," *New York Times*, January 19, 2014, SR1.

21. George A. Gonzalez, *Urban Sprawl, Global Warming, and the Empire of Capital* (Albany: State University of New York Press, 2009); Adrian Parr, *The Wrath of Capital: Neoliberalism and Climate Change Politics* (New York: Columbia University Press, 2013);

Hiroko Tabuchi, "The Banks Putting Rain Forests in Peril," *New York Times*, December 4, 2016, BU1.

22. George A. Gonzalez, *The Politics of* Star Trek: *Justice, War, and the Future* (New York: Palgrave Macmillan, 2015), 167–68.

FOUR

Grievance Studies

The term "grievance studies" has recently been coined.[1] It is cast and taken as an epithet of identity politics and the vast literature associated with it. While the phrase *grievance studies* is highly politicized, I would respectfully submit that there is evidence in the identity politics literature to support the idea that proponents of such politics seek out (even concoct) instances when minorities are putatively aggrieved. My point is certainly not to argue that minorities have achieved equality, or anything of the sort. Nevertheless, there may indeed be a bias among identity politics scholars/advocates to approach advancements in ethnic (race) and gender relations cynically—even unduly downplaying any such advances.

My argument centers on the broadcast iterations of the *Star Trek* franchise. This franchise arguably holds the broadest audience in all of popular culture. Thus, it is an important terrain of identity politics—with prominent critics charging that the franchise contains negative ethnic (racial) biases. *Star Trek* in fact takes a strong and lucid antiracist stance. Moreover, the franchise indicates that racism is linked to class oppression. In *Star Trek*'s utopian future class oppression no longer exists.

The Next Generation series (1987–1994), reflecting the resurgent nationalism of the Reagan Revolution,[2] does convey a racialist politics—i.e., the idea that nations and cultures are permanently cleaved into discrete entities.[3] This racialist outlook dominates the later *Star Trek* series *Enterprise*. The franchise should be read as both depicting and critiquing racialist thinking. Racialist thinking that apparently motivates identity politics scholarship—as indicated by the treatment of the *Star Trek* franchise.

STAR TREK AS LIBERATING TEXT

In asking why is the *Star Trek* franchise so entertaining to so many, we are engaging public opinion at the deepest levels. The Federation, across all of *Star Trek*'s platforms, is a secular (at times antireligion) interstellar institution that is classless, and predicated on the total absence of gender/ ethnic biases. In this way the franchise is based on reason (i.e., full and total equality).

Nevertheless, *Star Trek* is a work of art and artistic choices must be made—for better or for worse. Critics have seized on some of these choices to make what amount to superficial readings of the *Star Trek* text, thereby obfuscating the truly progressive/liberating/analytical elements of the franchise. Perhaps the most notable of *Star Trek*'s critics is Daniel Bernardi—who holds that the original series and *The Next Generation* are hopelessly marred by gender, ethnic, and sexual orientation biases.[4] Bernardi makes much of the fact that Lt. Uhura (the one African American bridge officer in the original series) is reduced to a bit role; that the Klingons are dark-skinned; *Next Generation* caregiver roles are assigned to women; and on neither of the first two *Star Trek* series are there any gay/lesbian characters.

In criticizing the Uhura character Bernardi is minimizing the fact that the original *Enterprise* (in the late 1960s) had a black, female bridge officer. That Uhura had a minimal role in the show's plots is neither here nor there—as a true racist stance would never afford a bridge officer position to an African American. Also noteworthy is the fact that an African American actor (in the original series) plays one of the Federation's leading scientific minds.[5]

Bernardi is correct that the Klingons (in *Next Generation*) are a political trope, but not one that reflects American race politics, per se—as he claims. The Klingons, Romulans, and Cardassians represent peoples of the less-developed world—as discussed elsewhere.[6]

What is truly amazing about Bernardi's assertion of racism directed against the *Next Generation* is his treatment of the characters Geordi Laforge, Worf, and Guinan (all played by African American actors). These characters are admirable—of the highest intelligence, fortitude, and integrity. Nevertheless, Bernardi dismisses them because they are putatively disconnected from their history: he holds that at the core of the *Next Generation* "is a Western and white standard."[7] It is unclear how Bernardi expects African Americans on the *Enterprise* to behave. Should they be speaking creole English (*ebonics*)? An obvious message would be that African Americans, in spite of equal educational and social opportunities, cannot master standard English.

Bernardi inappropriately homes in on what are essentially artistic choices and makes a broader (ultimately) unsustainable claim that *Next Generation* is profoundly racist. He makes hay of the fact that Captain

Picard is played by Patrick Stewart and that Worf is a subordinate officer (a lieutenant commander). In misplaced (racist[?]) language, Bernardi makes the following distastefully worded observation: Worf "is trained and domesticated, becoming . . . a trusted officer who faithfully protects the *Enterprise* and its white captain."[8] Bernardi cannot see beyond the skin tone of Picard and Worf to analyze their actual relationship—one built on professionalism and mutual respect (even admiration).

Bernardi similarly makes a mountain out of a mole hill by pointing out that a being that is conveyed as an evolutionary advancement is glowing white (*Next Generation*—"Transfigurations" 1990), while the beings from which all humanoids evolved have a tone that is tinged brown (*Next Generation*—"The Chase" 1993): "What is striking about 'Lucy' [the representation of the original humanoid species] is that the common ancestor to the bipeds of the universe is brown. Though dark or even colored is not where we're going . . . it is apparently where we come from."[9] Bernardi goes on: "the course of evolution, of advancement and sophistication, is literally and metaphorically, physically and socially, white . . . that's . . . *The Next Generation's* version of the promised land."[10] If the special effects designers had made "Lucy" a little whiter or the advanced being darker, maybe we could have been spared Bernardi's pseudo-racist rhetoric. I imagine, however, Bernardi would have something inappropriate/sardonic to say if Lucy were lily-white.

Perhaps what is most baffling about Bernardi's approach to *Star Trek* is while he is focusing on the superficial (e.g., Picard's and Worf's skin tones), he elides the universality communicated in "Transfigurations" and "The Chase." In "Transfigurations," for instance, the alien that is going through a metamorphosis to a higher state of existence comments positively on the heterogeneous composition of the *Enterprise* crew: "Truly remarkable. . . . They're all so different from one another yet they work together freely." The original humanoid species (in "The Chase") was very highly advanced (even with their tanned skin tone): "Life evolved on my planet before all others in this part of the galaxy. We left our world, explored the stars." Lucy preaches solidarity and unity—emphasizing that all humanoids share a common genetic basis:

> Our scientists seeded the primordial oceans of many worlds, where life was in its infancy. The seed codes directed your evolution toward a physical form resembling ours. This body you see before you, which is, of course, shaped as yours is shaped, for you are the end result. . . . It was our hope that you would have to come together in fellowship and companionship to hear this message [sent from the past in the form of Lucy]. And if you can see and hear me, our hope has been fulfilled. You are a monument, not to our greatness, but to our existence. That was our wish, that you too would know life, and would keep alive our memory. There is something of us in each of you, and so, something of you in each other. Remember us.

Lucy's message had a positive effect on a Romulan officer present during her speech. After everyone returns to their ship, he contacts Captain Picard: "It would seem that we are not completely dissimilar after all, in our hopes, or in our fears"—in spite of the current Romulan/Federation geopolitical competition. Picard: "Yes." Romulan: "Well, then. Perhaps, one day"—we can unify. Picard: "One day." Bernardi is too caught up in a game of *gotcha* to meaningfully engage the *Star Trek* text and its political/social implications.

Bernardi again focuses on the superficial when he criticizes the fact that leading female characters in *Next Generation* hold caregiver roles on the *Enterprise*. Deanna Troi is the ship's counselor and Beverly Crusher is the ship's doctor: "As in the original *Star Trek*, women in *The Next Generation* are consistently positioned as either helpers or fetishized objects. This is the case with both Dr. Crusher and Counselor Troi—their Federation jobs are supportive of their role as nurturers. The doctor and the counselor rarely give orders and almost always serve men."[11] (In drawing his criticisms Bernardi fails to mention the female character of Tasha Yar, who during the first season of *Next Generation* was head of security.) Firstly, in spite of Bernardi's judgmental tone, there's nothing wrong with women (or men) being nurturers, nor with women taking orders from men. Secondly, Bernardi puts forth no effort whatsoever to discuss the content of the Crusher or Troi characters (at this point nothing in his hackneyed treatment of *Star Trek* surprises me). Crusher is not simply a nurturer but the ship's head doctor—hence, more than taking orders from men she oversees medical care for the entire ship (a position of great responsibility and [one would imagine] prestige). Troi is not solely *Enterprise*'s counselor (its chief psychologist) (again a position in-and-of-itself of importance), but she is the Captain's close advisor (her sage advice is regularly instrumental to the plot). Moreover, Troi in the episode "Disaster" (1991—*Next Generation*) takes command of the ship and saves the day. In pondering the treatment of women in *Next Generation* it is important to note that female actors were frequently cast to play the roles of researchers; admirals; political leaders; and other positions of significant stature. Thus, the decision to cast female characters as ship's doctor and counselor amount to nothing more than artistic choices, and, most importantly, viewers watching the *Next Generation* would see women acting as decision-makers; learned scientists; key advisors; and holding positions of great authority.

Significantly, Bernardi published his book on race and gender in the *Star Trek* franchise in 1998. By this time *Deep Space Nine* and *Voyager* were already running for years. (*Deep Space Nine* began airing in 1993 and *Voyager* in 1995 [until 2001]). In *Deep Space Nine* the commanding officer is an African American male, with the first officer and science officer played by women. The starship *Voyager* is captained by a women. Bernardi makes no comment on these shows or characters. Apparently, he and his publisher didn't let anything get in the way of their myopic, captious approach toward *Star Trek.*

Bernardi and critics of his ilk[12] are on stronger ground when they fault *Star Trek* for lacking openly LGBT characters. Efforts are made by *Star Trek*'s creators to favorably, thoughtfully treat LGBT issues—e.g., *Next Generation* "The Outcast" (1992)—where on a homosexual world it is heterosexuals that suffer persecution. In the 1995 *Deep Space Nine* episode "Rejoined" one of the lead characters of the show does have a lesbian tryst. Nevertheless, it is painfully glaring in "The Host" (1991—*Next Generation*) when Dr. Crusher rejects the symbiont she has fallen in love with when it turns up in a female body—even though she earlier made love with the symbiont while it was in two different male bodies (one of them *Enterprise*'s First Officer William Riker).

David Greven, in his outstanding book *Gender and Sexuality in* Star Trek, makes a very interesting observation on the sexual orientation politics of *Star Trek.* Greven holds that while the *Star Trek* franchise (prior to *Star Trek: Discovery*) lacks LGBT characters, the franchise nonetheless presents a positive picture for the LGBT community. Graven's argument is that at the center of the *Star Trek* franchise is the claim that non-biological family relations are just as valid and fulfilling as relations informed by biology or marriage. This is particularly important for the LGBT community as historically its members were regularly estranged from their biological families—and given the fact that they were (historically) legally prohibited from forming new families (i.e., denied the right to marry and adopt). Graven points to the fact that the relationship between Kirk, Spock, and McCoy is as vital and emotionally intimate as any relationship conveyed on American television (perhaps more so). A similar argument can be made of all *Star Trek* series—where few characters are married or have children and same sex friendships are the norm. Graven (who makes the point in his book that he is gay himself) comes very close (in my estimation) to holding that the addition of LGBT characters in the *Star Trek* franchise would have been overkill (artistically speaking)—as the franchise is dominated by vibrant (nonbiological) relationships.[13]

STAR TREK AND RACE

Daniel Bernardi, as noted above, takes issue with the fact that the character of Lt. Uhuru (of the original series—played by an Afro actor) was limited to a supporting role in the original series.[14] André M. Carrington in *Speculative Blackness: The Future of Race in Science Fiction* takes a similarly negative tone with Uhuru's role on *Star Trek* as mostly a supporting character: "In light of the possibility for exterior adventures, the confinement of [Uhura] to the bridge relegated her diversifying function to a 'domestic' sphere, leaving her 'home' while adventures 'away' remained the province of the series's male leads."[15] The fact that the show was mostly centered on the characters of Kirk, Spock, and McCoy amounts to nothing more than artistic choices, and efforts to identify sinister motives in these choices is entirely cynical as well as misplaced. The presence of Uhura and other actors with Afro backgrounds on the original *Star Trek* are noteworthy (because as Carrington notes elsewhere in his book) racism in the science fiction genre has historically been manifest by denying the existence of people of color.

Bernardi's and Carrington's treatment of Uhura is significant in that their criticisms are at cross purposes. Bernardi faults the *Star Trek* franchise because it represents "a Western and white standard."[16] Yet when Uhura's quarters in "The Tholian Web" (1968—original series) have African-theme accouterments (featuring, for instance, a zebra skin bed spread) Carrington denounces this because he holds it equates people with an Afro background with "primitivism."[17] As already noted, it is unclear how the likes of Bernardi or Carrington expect Afro peoples on the *Enterprise* to behave.

Perhaps what is most glaring in Bernardi's and Carrington's treatment of the identity politics of the *Star Trek* franchise is the fact that neither make any comment on the original series episode "Let That Be Your Last Battlefield" (1969)—an episode that is explicitly antiracist. The *Enterprise* crew comes into contact with an alien race that is half white and half black, but part of the population is white on the right side and the other is white on the left side. The *Enterprise* crew cannot fathom that such a trivial difference would be politically, socially significant for anyone—much less fuel the intense hatred and violence that the two alien individuals on board the *Enterprise* direct toward one another (each one from the different ethnic groups). In the end we learn that the racism of this species resulted in its destruction.

It is significant that in the denouement of the episode Uhura proclaims that the behavior of these aliens "doesn't make any sense." She resides in a world of ethnic equality and fairness and cannot understand how people could hate so profoundly over something like skin tone—of course, viewers in the 1960s could. Spock, a Vulcan who works among humans, is similarly incredulous: "To expect sense from two mentalities of such extreme viewpoints is not logical."

Returning to the issue of expunging or ignoring the existence of Afro people in science fiction, if we take this as a marker of racism then Bernardi's 1998 book qualifies. The title of Bernardi's book is Star Trek *and History: Race-ing toward a White Future*. Despite having such a title, Bernardi in his book (as already observed) fails to discuss *Deep Space Nine*.

Carrington notes that "though it was on the air at the time of [Bernardi's] publication, [Bernardi] omits any substantive discussion of the significance of *Deep Space Nine*."[18] Interestingly, this does not stop Carrington from praising him: "Bernardi's work ably explains how the original

Star Trek and *The Next Generation* envision a future beyond racism while still falling prey to the shortcomings of the liberal discourse that produced them."[19] Bernardi minimizes the character of Uhura (as noted above). Additionally, Bernardi minimizes *The Next Generation* characters of Geordi Laforge, Worf, and Guinan (all played by African American actors). Carrington doesn't bother to discuss them.

EMPIRE AND RACISM

Carrington makes the following unfounded claim: "*Star Trek* is a discovery narrative, imagining a new age of exploration modeled on European colonial expeditions."[20] Original series episodes are perhaps the most powerful and clear-throated critiques of empire and colonialism in all of popular culture: "Mirror, Mirror" (1967), "Arena" (1967), "Private Little War" (1968), "A Piece of the Action" (1968), "The Paradise Syndrome" (1968), "Patterns of Force"(1968), and "Friday's Child" (1967). All these episodes to one degree or another take aim at colonialism and empire. As an anti-imperialist tract, "Mirror, Mirror" is particularly noteworthy.[21]

"Mirror, Mirror," discussed above, opens with a discussion between Kirk and the leader of the "Halkans" (named "Tharn"). The Halkans refuse to allow the Federation to mine the dilithium crystals on their planet because "dilithium crystals represent awesome power. Wrongful use of that power, even to the extent of the taking of one life, would violate our history of total peace." Kirk asks "When may we resume discussion?" Tharn: "The council will meditate further, but do not be hopeful of any change." Tharn adds: "Captain, you do have the might to force the crystals from us, of course." Kirk: "But we won't."

Through a technical glitch, the *Enterprise* landing party is transported to an alternate universe. The *Enterprise* exists in this alternate universe, but instead of the Federation the political authority is the "Empire"—where "behavior and discipline" is "brutal, savage." While in the Federation universe the *Enterprise* only pursues peaceful means with the Halkans, in the Empire universe Kirk is "ordered to annihilate the Halkans unless they comply. *No alternative*." "Mirror, Mirror" is an explicit rejection/critique of military intervention into other societies—particularly for purposes of controlling natural resources. A censure that can be issued to the United States of the Cold War era.

Carrington's use of the phrase "European colonial expeditions" is on its face racist. Firstly, in world history Europeans were certainly not the only peoples to engage in colonialism. Hence, Carrington vilifies Europeans as the only ones guilty of the sins of colonialism. Secondly, Carrington's description of the *Star Trek* text as based on "a new age of exploration modeled on European colonial expeditions" can be read as marginalizing people of color's role in *Star Trek*'s narrative "to go where no one has gone before." This is a European affair and people of color are only pawns in this project. This casts the characters of Uhura, LaForge, Worf, etc., in a subservient and demeaning light.

CLASS AND RACISM

What is most significant and important about *Star Trek*'s antiracism is that its creators seek to identify the causes of institutional racism. Racism is a function of class oppression. In the *Deep Space Nine* episode "Far Beyond the Stars" (1998) Captain Sisko is transported back in time—to New York City in the 1950s, where he is a staff writer for a science fiction magazine. African Americans are publicly denied any space in the genre during this time, and Sisko's personae (Benny Russell) is asked not to show up to work the day the magazine is set to take the staff picture (as is the sole woman writer on staff). Sisko/Russell gets inspired to write the story of the Deep Space Nine station, along with its African American captain. Very importantly, the entirety of the staff, along with the managing editor, support Russell and press to have his story published. In the end, the (unseen) owner of the magazine decides to "pulp" the issue that month. It is made clear that he rather lose the money than distribute a story featuring a black character. In the original series episode "Patterns of Force" the argument is made that racism is a tool used by elites to maintain societal stability: "Why do the Nazis hate Zeons?" "Because without us to hate, there'd be nothing to hold them together." "Day of the Dove" (1968—original series) has an alien forcing the crew of the *Enterprise* to engage in "race hatred." "Plato's Stepchildren" (1968—original series) casts a planet's powerful elites as sadists who enjoy inflicting sexual and physical abuse. Viewers see Uhura forced into kissing someone and threatened with a whip.

The original series episode "Cloud Minders"(1969) depicts a society (the planet of Ardana) where torture technology ("the rays")—and racism—are used to maintain/stabilize a caste system. (Ardana is a seeming stand-in for South Africa.) In effective imagery the political/economic/social realities of the planet are portrayed—with the privileged/governing caste living a life of aesthetic splendor in a "cloud city" ("Stratos") floating in the heavens; on the (barren) planet surface are where the laboring classes (referred to as "Troglytes") live—working the mines (extracting "zenite"). The residents of Stratos are fair-skinned and fair-haired and partake in the high arts. The Troglytes are dark-haired, dark-skinned, and unwashed.

"The rays" are deployed in an effort to break a political movement in opposition to the governing regime. A prisoner is pressed to provide the names of the putative leaders of the mining caste's rebellion: "You still refuse to disclose the names of the other Disrupters." "There are no Disrupters!" "Very well, if you prefer the rays." She screams in agony, discomforting onlookers. Spock, in his famous calm, equanimous voice, observes that "Violence in reality is quite different from theory."

> **Droxine**: But what else can [Troglytes] understand, Mister Spock?
>
> **Spock**: All the little things you and I understand and expect from life, such as equality, kindness, justice.
>
> **Plasus**: Troglytes are not like Stratos dwellers, Mister Spock. They're a conglomerate of inferior species.

Star Trek makes clear that in the future class oppression for humans and Earth is no longer an issue. Beginning in the late 1980s *Star Trek* starts to base its plots on racialist thinking. The original series was produced in the aftermath of the international solidarity in the fight against fascism and during the social justice politics of the New Deal and the Great Society. Later *Star Trek* was produced during the politically conservative Reagan Revolution, when cynicism set in about social justice and nationalism was resurgent. Later *Star Trek* both conveys and critiques the racialist thinking that became predominate as part of the Reagan Revolution.

Apart from the conservative turn in American politics in the 1980s, racialist reasoning is also promoted by identity politics advocates. In the case of the *Star Trek* franchise, by falsely tarring it as unfair to ethnic minorities, women and LGBTQ *Star Trek*'s identity politics critics are arguing that even this self-proclaimed progressive franchise replicates the biases and grievances that serve to permanently divide identity groups.

RACIALIST IDEATION IN *STAR TREK*

Star Trek is notable and laudable for its treatment, denunciation of racism. Beginning with *Star Trek* of the late 1980s, nevertheless, the franchise shifts to what can be labeled racialist reasoning. In other words, that there are insurmountable, even genetic, differences between cultures. In "The Icarus Factor" (1989—*Next Generation*) the point is explicitly made by the steadfastly objective Lt. Comdr. Data that "there is, of course, a genetic predisposition toward hostility among all Klingons." The Romulans in the *Next Generation* are cast in broad brushed racialist terms as "violent beyond description"; also "their belief in their own superiority is beyond arrogance."[22] While the galaxy of *Star Trek* in the 1980s is permanently cleaved into different racialist societies (the Romulans, the Klingons, the Cardassians, etc.), there are no specific claims of racial superiority. All these cultures are the technological equal of the Federation—the quintessential modernist society.

Nevertheless, *Star Trek* does indicate that racialism does result in xenophobia. The xenophobia of the Klingons is evident when Worf is chided for bringing "*outsiders* [i.e., humans] to our Great Hall."[23] In another instance, one Klingon is opposed to another Klingon marrying a non-Klingon: "She believes that by bringing aliens into our families we risk losing our identity as Klingons." This is acknowledged as "a prejudiced, xenophobic view."[24]

The racism in racialist reasoning is particularly evident in the *Next Generation* episode "Birthright" (1993). The action centers on a prison camp established by the Romulans over twenty years earlier to house a group of Klingons who could not return home. They were stigmatized by the fact that they were taken prisoner—Klingons are expected to fight to the death or commit suicide if captured. As an act of kindness, and at great sacrifice, a Romulan officer agrees to oversee the camp—otherwise the captured Klingons would be executed. Worf—whose father was falsely rumored to be at the camp—discovers it. He objects to an arrangement whereby Klingons live as prisoners of the Romulans—even though they are treated well; have complete freedom on the planet they reside on; have given birth to children; and share a strong sense of community. Worf, nevertheless, tells the Romulan camp commander (Tokath) that "you robbed the Klingons of who they were. *You dishonored them.*" Tokath, pointing to the irrationality of Worf's position, retorts: "By not slitting their throats when we found them unconscious?" Worf explicitly resorts to racialist thinking to justify his position: "I do not expect you to understand. *You are a Romulan.*" Hence, there is something *particular* about Klingons, and it is inscrutable to non-Klingons. Tokath explains "we've put aside the old hatreds. Here, Romulans and Klingons live in peace." Worf is unmoved: "Do not deceive yourself. These people are not happy here. I see the sadness in their eyes."

Worf adopts an openly hateful attitude when he comes to discover that a woman (Ba'el) he is romantically interested in is an offspring of one of the Klingon prisoners and a Romulan. Worf is kissing Ba'el, draws back her hair and sees her pointed ears (characteristic of Romulans). Outraged Worf exclaims "*You are Romulan*!" Unabashed in his racism, he asks with a tone of disgust: "*How could your mother mate with a Romulan?*" He declares "*it is an obscenity*!" Fully venting his hate, Worf tells Ba'el: "Romulans are *treacherous, deceitful*. They are without honor." Ba'el: "My father is a good man. He is kind, and generous. There is nothing dishonorable about him."

EARTH-VULCAN RELATIONS IN *ENTERPRISE*

Racialist reasoning is at the core of the *Star Trek* television series *Enterprise*. Perhaps the most salient aspect of the *Enterprise* narrative is that unlike in the original series where the Vulcans and Earthlings are part of the same Federation polity, in this series Earth and Vulcan have an uneasy relationship and form two discrete political formations. *Enterprise* indicates that with racialism as politically dominant this propels Earthlings toward xenophobia. Additionally, as seen through the Xindi (described below) racialism in the modern era can lead to planetary destruction.

Star Trek: First Contact (1996) (the movie) is predicated on a WE/THEY distinction. The action of the movie takes place in the year 2063. The Borg go back in Earth's history to prevent humanity's first contact with the Vulcans. This initial exposure to an alien culture occurs because Zephran Cochrane conducts humanity's first successful warp drive experiment. ("Warp speed" represents a speed faster than light.) When the Vulcans detect Cochrance's ship achieving warp speed they decide to introduce themselves to earthlings—"first contact." In this iteration (*First Contact*) of *Star Trek*'s historiography of Earth in 2063 humanity is in what is referred to in the movie as a "Second Dark Age."[25] What rallies humanity from its disarray is its contact with the Vulcans: "*It unites humanity in a way no one ever thought possible when they realize they're not alone in the universe*." This is consonant with Samuel Huntington's racialist *clash of civilizations* argument, where he holds that "for peoples seeking identity and reinventing ethnicity, *enemies are essential*."[26]

Therefore, the political foundation of humanity in the mid-twenty-first century is the WE/THEY dichotomy—with the Vulcans serving as "They"—and this is the basis of *Enterprise* (set in the twenty-second century, whereas the original series and *Discovery* are set in the twenty-third century and *Next Generation*; *Deep Space Nine*; *Voyager* in the twenty-fourth). In *Enterprise* conflict/competition with the Vulcans does occur. "The Forge" (2004), "Awakening" (2004), and the "Kir'Shara" (2004) is a three episode story arc whereby Earth's embassy on Vulcan is bombed, killing Admiral Forrest (Captain Archer's mentor), and the *Enterprise* crew gets swept up in internal Vulcan religious and political strife—with an effort made against Captain Archer's life; and the *Enterprise* and Vulcan military ships coming to a face-off. In the denouement we learn that elements within the Vulcan government were behind the bombing of the Earth embassy, and that a faction still in the government wants to pull the planet toward a political/military alliance with the Romulans. An intention ominously threatening to Earth as it suggests the formation of a Vulcan-Romulan civilization (they are the same ethnicity).

Especially telling for a politics based on competing *civilizations*, *Enterprise* conveys Earth's polity as afflicted with xenophobia and racism. The series concludes in 2005 and the penultimate episode centers on the group "Terra Prime" (episode title). Initially, this organization is described as xenophobic: "They want to stop all contact with alien species." "They believe it's corrupting our way of life." Later, we learn that Terra

Prime is racist: "This is an alien-human hybrid. Living proof of what will happen if we allow ourselves to be submerged in an interstellar coalition. Our genetic heritage. . . ." "That child is a cross-breed freak. How many generations before our genome is so diluted that the word human is nothing more than a footnote in some medical text?" The leader of Terra Prime declares "I'm returning Earth to its rightful owners." Referring to signs of broad sympathy for Terra Prime and its agenda, the Vulcan Ambassador Soval notes: "The fact that [Terra Prime] has the support of so many of your people is . . . troubling."

Of great significance for a discussion based on Huntington's vision of world politics informed by the idea of conflictive *civilizations*, is the Xindi—introduced in *Enterprise*. The Xindi are the former inhabitants of the planet Xindi. The Xindi are cleaved into five distinct *civilizations*, with each civilization corresponding to a distinct species: one insectoid, one humanoid, aquatic, ape-like, and reptilian. As a result of their competition, the Xindi destroyed their planet: "The war went on for nearly a hundred years. . . . The insectoids and reptilians detonated massive explosions beneath the eight largest seismic fissures. I'd like to think they didn't realize how devastating the result would be."[27]

CONCLUSION

As arguably the most popular and politically modern text in the world, the *Star Trek* franchise (its broadcast iterations) serves as a saliently important political theory corpus. Critics of this corpus hold that it depicts negative ethnic biases. Such criticisms are without merit, as the *Star Trek* text is explicitly antiracist. An innovation for a popular culture medium, *Star Trek* links racism and class oppression. The utopia of *Star Trek* eliminates class and racism.

Why would critics falsely seek to stigmatize the *Star Trek* text as somehow racist, sexist? Importantly, these critics are on the nominal left and self-proclaimed champions of ethnic and gender minorities. Their attack on *Star Trek* is ostensibly motivated by the belief, argument that social, political progress in society is not possible. Thus, even a highly successful television franchise that claims the mantle of social progress nonetheless has to be marred by racism, gender bias.

Star Trek of the late 1980s adopts the racialism of the Reagan Revolution, with the *Star Trek* series (*Enterprise*) explicitly predicated on racialist politics. In depicting this racialism *Star Trek* offers key critiques of racialist politics—namely, that such politics result in xenophobia. Significantly, *Star Trek* (through the parable of the Xindi) indicates that racialism can result in planetary destruction in the modern era. The promoters of *grievance studies* arguably help to create and reinforce racialist politics—holding that even progressive art (*Star Trek*) replicate (in the worst way possible) racialist cleavages.

NOTES

1. Jennifer Schuessler, "With Canine Sex and Hooters, Pranks Jab at Academic Papers," *New York Times*, October 5, 2018, A1.
2. Jeffrey L. Chidester and Paul Kengor, eds., *Reagan's Legacy in a World Transformed* (Cambridge, MA: Harvard University Press, 2015); Doug Rossinow, *The Reagan Era: A History of the 1980s* (New York: Columbia University Press, 2015).
3. Samuel P. Huntington, *The Clash of Civilizations and the Remaking of World Order* (New York: Simon & Schuster, 1996 [2011]).
4. Daniel Leonard Bernardi, Star Trek *and History: Race-ing toward a White Future* (New Brunswick: Rutgers University Press, 1998).
5. "The Ultimate Computer," 1968.
6. George A. Gonzalez, *The Politics of* Star Trek*: Justice, War, and the Future* (New York: Palgrave Macmillan, 2015), chap. 3.
7. Bernardi, Star Trek *and History*, 130.
8. Ibid., 134.
9. Ibid., 127.
10. Ibid., 136.
11. Ibid., 116.
12. E.g., Robin Roberts, *Sexual Generations:* "Star Trek: The Next Generation" *and Gender* (Chicago: University of Illinois Press, 1999).
13. David Greven, *Gender and Sexuality in* Star Trek*: Allegories of Desire in the Television Series and Films* (Jefferson, NC: MacFarland, 2009).
14. Bernardi, Star Trek *and History*.
15. André M. Carrington, *Speculative Blackness: The Future of Race in Science Fiction* (Minneapolis: University of Minnesota Press, 2016), 73–74.
16. Bernardi, Star Trek *and History*, 130.
17. Carrington, *Speculative Blackness*, 74.
18. Carrington, *Speculative Blackness*, 160.
19. Carrington, *Speculative Blackness*, 160.
20. Carrington, *Speculative Blackness*, 161.
21. Gonzalez, *The Politics of* Star Trek.
22. *Next Generation*—"The Neutral Zone," 1988.
23. *Next Generation*—"Sins of the Father," 1990.
24. *Deep Space Nine*—"You Are Cordially Invited," 1997.
25. http://www.st-minutiae.com/academy/literature329/fc.txt.
26. Huntington, *The Clash of Civilizations*, 20, emphasis added.
27. *Enterprise*—"The Shipment," 2003.

FIVE

The Metaphysics Debate

Ronald E. Osborn in *Humanism and the Death of God: Searching for the Good after Darwin, Marx, and Nietzsche* casts the state of metaphysics scholarship, philosophy as a dichotomy between atheism and religious epistemology.[1] Osborn identifies Darwin, Marx, and Nietzsche as carrying the banner for atheism. Osborn conflates these thinkers (and atheism) with analytic philosophy (i.e., *material realism*)—the idea that reality does not extend beyond the empirical.[2] This is a misnomer in the case of Marx, who philosophized in the tradition of German philosopher Georg Hegel[3]—who explicitly held that reality extends beyond the empirical (i.e., the Absolute, a fifth dimension where normative values are embedded).[4]

Osborn, thinkers of his ilk, as well as analytic philosophers, may dismiss Hegel's philosophizing about the Absolute by holding that his thinking has no particular following. Given that Hegel's writings are obscure to those outside of academia, his theory on metaphysics is not worth considering along with the great traditions of religion and atheism. This overlooks the metaphysical theories, arguments of the *Star Trek* franchise—arguably the most popular television franchise in history. *Star Trek* (its broadcast iterations) is directly predicated on Hegelian reasoning,[5] as well as on that of Karl Marx.[6] Many of the fans of *Star Trek* embrace it with a religious fervor[7]—indicating that viewers do identify the metaphysics underlying the franchise and are drawn to its metaphysical claims.

Osborn aptly holds that analytic philosophy (or what he labels atheism) offers at best thin conceptions of morality and ethics. Whereas *atheism* does not extend much morally, ethically beyond limited, contextual fairness claims,[8] Osborn avers that religion proffers robust, thick notions of justice. He explains that religion yields a comprehensive rights regime derived from prophetic epistemology. Osborn is specifically critical of

Karl Marx's dismissive attitude toward the idea of rights as a means of justice—linking this attitude to the criminality of the Stalin(ist) regime of the former Soviet Union.[9]

Star Trek is critical of prophetic political reasoning (theocracy) because it inherently stunts the human intellect (as well as society), and is ultimately destabilizing and dangerous. Additionally, *Star Trek* shows that a rights regime is not necessarily consonant with justice, fairness, or even freedom—as metapolitics a rights regime can be about maintaining political stability for a profoundly unjust social order. A rights regime encourages lies and other unethical behavior.

Paralleling Hegel and (especially) Marx, *Star Trek* indicates a justice regime as the only means to establish a society that is just—one that is classless and free of ethnic and gender biases. A justice regime is the result of the *progressive dialectic* derived from the *absolute*.

THE ABSOLUTE IN *STAR TREK*

The *Star Trek* text rejects both analytic philosophy and prophetic reasoning, as well as embraces Hegelian metaphysics, in the *Voyager* episode "Sacred Ground" (1996). In this episode a direct reference to the existence of "spirits" is made—a term Hegel himself would use to denote something beyond material existence (e.g., the physical laws [spirits] of gravity, conservation, thermal dynamics; also, the spirits of love, morality, happiness, etc.). During the episode, the following is said to Janeway: "Mathematics. I can see why you enjoyed it. Solve a problem, get an answer. The answer's either right or wrong. It's very *absolute*." A veiled reference to Hegel's philosophy? Indicative of Hegelian reasoning the following point is made: "Real is such a relative term." Janeway's materialist (i.e., analytic philosophy) thinking is described in the following: "That would be nice and quantifiable for you, wouldn't it. If the spirits were something you could see and touch and scan with your little devices." Overtly critiquing Kantian rationalism,[10] the following is said to Janeway: "There you go again, always looking for a rational explanation. Well there isn't one."

The action of "Sacred Ground" centers on the fact that *Voyager* crew member, Kes, becomes incapacitated when she comes into contact with an "energy field." *Voyager*'s doctor is unable to bring Kes out of her coma and she's on the verge of death. Unable to find a scientific explanation for the field or Kes's condition, Captain Janeway is forced to appeal to the "monks" that oversee the energy field. They consider it a manifestation of their deities—the *Ancestral Spirits*. In order to save Kes, Janeway is told "that the only thing that matters is finding your connection to the spirits." Importantly, this connection is not found through a prophetic text. In the end, it is only when Janeway accepts that something beyond material reality exists (i.e., the *Ancestral Spirits*) that Kes is revived.

Moreover, in "Transfigurations" (1990—*Next Generation*), *Star Trek* makes the explicit argument that those with the appropriate Zen could fully comprehend the absolute. "John Doe," as he regains his memories and bearings, is finally able to transform into seemingly the *whole*—the absolute. John: "my species is on the verge of a wondrous evolutionary change. A transmutation beyond our physical being. I am the first of my kind to approach this metamorphosis." "My people are about to embark upon a new realm, a new plane of existence." The character is cast as possessing a quality of peace and kindness. Dr. Crusher to John: "I don't believe you're capable of harming any[one].")

In contrast to John Doe, who seemingly achieves the ideal balance between emotion and reason (or Zen) and ostensibly comes to completely know (perhaps become) the absolute, Commander Sunad of Zalkon—who demands John be killed—is dominated by "fear" of social change. ("The Zalkonians are afraid of John.") They are fearful that John's transformation is subversive. Sunad charges that John "is a disruptive influence. He spreads lies. He encourages dissent. He disturbs the natural order of our society." (John: Zalkon's "leaders . . . claimed we were dangerous so they destroyed anyone who exhibited the signs of the transfiguration.")

Sunad's fear prevents him from embracing the fact that John has achieved a higher plane of existence, and when John offers him the knowledge of this existence ("Let me show you") Sunad rejects it ("Don't touch me!"). Sunad "feels personally threatened by John." Thus, Sunad's instrumental reason[11] (i.e., his desire for political authority; high social status; and social/political stability as an end unto itself) prevents him from literally seeing/knowing the absolute.

Star Trek indicates that the Zen required to know the absolute is achieved through honesty, selflessness, and a commitment to intellectual, scientific discovery/knowledge. These are the values at the core of the Federation. Captain Picard declares that "The first duty of every Starfleet officer is to the *truth*. Whether it's scientific truth, or historical truth, or personal truth. *It is the guiding principle upon which Starfleet is based*" (*Next Generation*—"The First Duty" 1992).[12] (Starfleet is the military institution of the Federation.) Indicating the selfless politics and economics of twenty-third-century humanity, Kirk (in the original series) explains to someone in the early twentieth-century New York City that "*Let me help*. A hundred years or so from now, I believe, a famous novelist will write a classic using that theme. He'll recommend those three words even over *I love you*" ("City on the Edge of Forever" 1967). In making the case for a federated interstellar political system to an audience of delegates of the would-be United Federation of Planets, Captain Archer emphasizes the overriding importance of space exploration and expanding scientific knowledge:

> Up until about a hundred years ago, there was one question that burned in every human, that made us study the stars and dream of traveling to them, Are we alone? Our generation is privileged to know the answer to that question. We are all explorers, driven to know what's over the horizon, what's beyond our own shores. And yet, the more I've experienced, the more I've learned that no matter how far we travel, or how fast we get there, the most profound discoveries are not necessarily beyond that next star. They're within us, woven into the threads that bind us, all of us, to each other. The final frontier begins in this hall. Let's explore it together. (*Enterprise*—"Terra Prime" 2005)

According to *Star Trek*, a society founded upon honesty, selflessness, and intellectual, scientific discovery/knowledge comes about through the rejection of capitalism and the replacement of the neoliberal world order—as explained in chapter 1. Thus, only through the rejection of instrumental reason as a philosophical/political foundation can a society achieve the absolute.

Rationality in *Star Trek*, as for Hegel, is found not in reducing the absolute to an object (a prophetic text), but in understanding the ontology of the absolute. *The Next Generation* episode "Justice" (1987) expressly rejects prophetic morality (divine rules) when one of the *Enterprise* crew violates a "law" handed down by the deity of the planet. The society and the deity demand that the divine rules be upheld to the letter, which would result in the execution of the *Enterprise* crew member. (The crew member unknowingly and accidentally violated a forbidden area.) In the face of prophetic strictures, Captain Picard argues to the deity "that there can be no justice so long as laws are absolute." First Officer Riker adds "when has justice ever been as simple as a rulebook?"

"Measure of a Man" (1989), a *Next Generation* episode, lucidly describes judicial proceedings as a dialectical process—ideally composed of countervailing forces—driving toward truth/justice. As part of a trial convened to determine Lt. Cmdr. Data's rights as an android, Captain Picard declares "The courtroom is a crucible. In it we burn away irrelevancies until we are left with a pure product, the truth for all time."

THEOCRACY IN *STAR TREK*

If rationality is engaging the dialectic of the absolute, then blunting an understanding or analysis of this dialectic (through prophecy) blunts human intellectual and social development. Two episodes from the original series explicitly point to political religion as barriers to social, political, economic, and intellectual progress: "The Return of the Archons" (1967) and "The Apple" (1967). "The Return of the Archons" focuses on a planet where a religious cult predominates—centered on the figure of "Landru." Almost everyone on the planet is an obedient follower of Landru. Those under his spell speak in overtly religious, evangelical terms: "He goes to joy, peace, and tranquility. He goes to meet Landru. Happiness is to all of us, blessed by Landru. . . . Blessed be the Body [i.e., the community of Landru followers], and health to all of its parts." The adherents of Landru are cast as vacuous drones. Spock observes: "The expression on that man's face. The mindlessness. Vacant contentment."

The religion of Landru is explicitly described as retrograde, as under his auspices society went "back to a simple time." Thus, the planet's society was highly advanced but it returned to a technological-level consonant with nineteenth-century small-town life, and has been in this state for six thousand years.

Kirk decides to destroy the machine that imposes the cult of Landru, and in so doing expressly holds that this religion is preventing the evolution of society. When Spock invokes the Prime Directive (the Federation policy of noninterference),[13] Kirk responds that the directive "refers to a living, growing culture. Do you think this one is?" Directly implying that political religion stifles autonomous thought and a vibrant, evolving society, Kirk (to the computer that upholds the cult of Landru): "Without creativity, there is no life. The body [i.e., community] dies." Spock adds: "Creativity is necessary for the health of the Body."

Star Trek again argues that political religion (prophetic reasoning) is an inherently socially, intellectually stunting phenomenon in "The Apple." Visiting the planet Gamma Trianguli VI, the *Enterprise* crew find that the inhabitants are content living a primitive life. They are sustained by an artificial intelligence also inhabiting the planet: "I just ran a check on the natives, and there's a complete lack of harmful bacteria in their systems, no decalcification, no degeneration of tissue, no arteriosclerosis. In simple terms, they're not growing old, and I can't tell you how old they are—20 years or 20,000 years." The natives provide the machine (Vaal) with energy (food) to maintain it. McCoy objects to this arrangement but Spock objects to applying human values to the situation, regarding it as "a splendid example of reciprocity":

> **McCoy**: It would take a computerized Vulcan mind, such as yours, to make that kind of a statement.
>
> **Spock**: Doctor, you insist on applying human standards to nonhuman cultures. Humans are only a tiny minority in this galaxy.
>
> **McCoy**: There are certain absolutes, and one of them is the right of humanoids to a free and unchained environment, the right to have conditions which permit growth.

Spock: Doctor, these people are healthy and they are happy. Whatever you choose to call it, this system works, despite your emotional reaction to it.

McCoy: It might work for you, Mr. Spock, but it doesn't work for me.

Kirk expresses a similar opinion in "This Side of Paradise" (1967—original series) when his crew opts under an alien influence for a bucolic and sedentary life: "Man stagnates if he has no ambition, no desire to be more than he is" (i.e., evolve socially, intellectually).

Kirk in the end decides to destroy Vaal arguing that it is preventing the inhabits of the planet from developing socially, economically, or even intellectually: "These people aren't living, they're existing. They don't create, they don't produce, they don't even think. They exist to service a machine [i.e., a god]." Kirk uses what can be viewed as Enlightenment rhetoric when assuring the natives that their lives will be better post-Vaal—in spite of the fact that the machine provided for all their needs: "You'll learn to build for yourselves, think for yourselves. . . . You'll like it, a lot." In the denouement an argument against religious paternalism (the natives worshiped Vaal) is posited (as biblical allegory is expressly invoked):

Spock: Captain, you are aware of the biblical story of Genesis.

Kirk: Yes, of course I'm aware of it. Adam and Eve tasted the apple and as a result were driven out of paradise.

Spock: Precisely, Captain, and in a manner of speaking, we have given the people of Vaal the apple, the knowledge of good and evil if you will, as a result of which they too have been driven out of paradise.

Despite Spock's claim that they drove the people of Vaal out of Eden, McCoy confidently holds "we put those people back on a normal course of social evolution." Thus, it is preferable to struggle for survival and develop your mind and society as a result (i.e., engage the absolute), than it is to live in comfort but in ignorance (in a stifled society).

More broadly, political religion (theocracy) is something to be avoided because it is extremely dangerous. "All Our Yesterdays" (1969) is an original series episode where Captain Kirk is transported back to the Puritan period, and comes close to being burned alive for being a "witch." When the *Enterprise* (in *Next Generation*) is involved in rekindling religious beliefs among a group of primitive people, the point is made "that religion could degenerate into inquisitions, holy wars, chaos"[14]—as groups (inspired by competing prophecies) compete for political dominance.

A RIGHTS REGIME AND JUSTICE

The (justice) dialectic of the absolute operates on the meta-level. Following from *Star Trek*, the absolute functions as a *progressive dialectic*—moving humanity toward a classless society, free of gender and ethnic biases.

An alternative to the progressive dialectic is a rights regime. As noted above, Osborn holds that rights derived from prophecy is the basis of justice, fairness, and freedom. A rights regime, however, can be consonant with empire and even slavery. This is depicted in the original series episode "Bread and Circuses" (1968).

The *Enterprise* crew comes upon a planet that is virtually identical to mid-twentieth Earth (America); except on this world the Roman Empire never collapsed and, instead, spans the entire planet. "A world ruled by emperors who can trace their line back 2,000 years to their own Julius and Augustus Caesars." The result is that slavery continues—in part because the slave system was reformed to maintain its stability: "Long ago, there were [slave] rebellions" but "with each century, the *slaves acquired more rights under the law*. They received rights to medicine, the right to government payments in their old age, and they slowly learned to be content." Spock: "Slavery evolving into an institution with guaranteed medical payments, old-age pensions." Hence, *rights* can be the carrot used to maintain a fundamentally unjust and repressive regime.

Moreover, in a regime where there are only rights, but no commitment to meta-justice (i.e., the progressive dialectic), it is logical/rational to maximize one's rights at the expense of others. This is outlined in the *Deep Space Nine* episode "Starship Down" (1995). Quark, a Ferengi—a species that elevates market ideology to a religion[15]—is caught padding expenses. He justifies his skulduggery by arguing that in a rights regime, where contracts are the prime basis for economic interactions, he assumes that everyone is cheating to maximize their profits (i.e., rights): "I cheated you. I cheat everyone. It's business. You see what you can get away with, and you've got to figure the other guy's doing the same to you."

CONCLUSION

Ronald E. Osborn, as noted above, in reviewing the field of metaphysics limits his discussion to atheism (analytic philosophy) and religion. He elides the metaphysics of the Hegelian absolute. Osborn presumably eschews a discussion of Hegelian metaphysics because it has no broad following. This would be a misplaced assumption, as *Star Trek* is expressly predicated on Hegelian reasoning, and this franchise has a following in the untold millions.

Star Trek extends Hegelian thought into the modern, contemporary period. Holding that justice, fairness, and freedom can only be achieved through a justice regime—resulting in a classless society, free of ethnic and gender biases (à la Karl Marx). It is by engaging the ontology of the absolute (and by implication the progressive dialectic) that humans individually and collectively advance. Prophetic reasoning and politics prevent intellectual and social development, and serves to destabilize society. Additionally, a rights regime derived from prophecy promotes unethical behavior and can be an instrument of a profoundly oppressive and unjust regime.

NOTES

1. Ronald E. Osborn, *Humanism and the Death of God: Searching for the Good after Darwin, Marx, and Nietzsche* (New York: Oxford University Press, 2017).
2. Hans-Johann Glock, *What Is Analytic Philosophy?* (New York: Cambridge University Press, 2008); Stephen P. Schwartz, *A Brief History of Analytic Philosophy: From Russell to Rawls* (West Sussex, UK: Wiley-Blackwell, 2012); Jan Westerhoff, *Reality: A Very Short Introduction* (New York: Oxford University Press, 2012); Ralph Wedgwood, *The Value of Rationality* (New York: Oxford University Press, 2017).
3. Peter Singer, *Marx: A Very Short Introduction* (New York: Oxford University Press, 2001); Gareth Stedman Jones, *Karl Marx: Greatness and Illusion* (Cambridge: Cambridge University Press, 2016); Tom Rockmore, *Marx's Dream: From Capitalism to Communism* (Chicago: University of Chicago Press, 2018).
4. Donald Phillip Verene, *Hegel's Absolute: An Introduction to Reading the Phenomenology of Spirit* (Albany: State University New York Press, 2007); Stephen Houlgate, *Hegel's "Phenomenology of Spirit": A Reader's Guide* (New York: Bloomsbury Academic, 2013); Brady Bowman, *Hegel and the Metaphysics of Absolute Negativity* (Cambridge: Cambridge University Press, 2015); James Kreines, *Reason in the World: Hegel's Metaphysics and Its Philosophical Appeal* (New York: Oxford University Press, 2015); Andrew Feenberg, *Technosystem: The Social Life of Reason* (Cambridge, MA: Harvard University Press, 2017).
5. George A. Gonzalez, *The Absolute and* Star Trek (New York: Palgrave Macmillan, 2017), *Popular Culture as Art and Knowledge* (Lanham, MD: Lexington Books, 2019), and *Popular Culture and the Political Values of Neoliberalism* (Lanham, MD: Lexington Books, 2019).
6. George A. Gonzalez, *The Politics of* Star Trek*: Justice, War, and the Future* (New York: Palgrave Macmillan, 2015).
7. Jon Wagner and Jan Lundeen, *Deep Space and Sacred Time:* Star Trek *in the American Mythos* (Westport, CT: Praeger, 1998); Jennifer E. Porter and Darcess L. McLaren, eds., Star Trek *and Sacred Ground: Explorations of* Star Trek*, Religion, and American Culture* (Albany: State University of New York Press, 1999).
8. John Rawls, *A Theory of Justice* (Cambridge, MA: Belknap, 1971); Stuart Hampshire, *Justice Is Conflict* (Princeton: Princeton University Press, 2000); Rainer Forst, *Contexts of Justice*, trans. John M. M. Farrell (Berkeley: University of California Press, 2002).
9. Osborn, *Humanism and the Death of God*, chap. 3.
10. In the *Critique of Pure Reason*, Kant argues that reason and empiricism can account for all phenomena. Immanuel Kant, *Critique of Pure Reason*, trans. Max Muller (New York: Penguin, 2008 [1781]).
11. Darrow Schecter, *The Critique of Instrumental Reason from Weber to Habermas* (New York: Bloomsbury Academic, 2012); Max Horkheimer, *Critique of Instrumental Reason*, trans. Matthew O'Connell (New York: Verso, 2013).
12. When Captain Kirk in *Star Trek: Into Darkness* (2013) is caught lying to Starfleet he is stripped of his captaincy.

13. A critique of U.S. foreign policy can be read into the Federation's *Prime Directive*. It is a policy of "Non-Interference" (first articulated in the original series), which expressly proscribes changing/influencing "the normal evolution" of non-Federation worlds ("A Piece of the Action" 1968). While not always upheld by the *Enterprise* crew, the Prime Directive establishes that the Federation is prohibited from giving advanced technology to non-Federation planets, as well as influencing the politics/economics of said planets ("The Apple" 1967; "Private Little War" 1968; "Friday's Child" 1967; "Bread and Circuses" 1968; "A Piece of the Action"). The Prime Directive would be directly at odds with Modernization Theory, embraced by foreign policy-makers in the White House during the 1960s. Modernization theory amounted to a Cold War strategy to share advanced technology and foster particular economic policies within the pro-Western countries of the *developing world* in an effort to solidify their position within the American-led camp. Michael E. Latham, *Modernization as Ideology: American Social Science and "Nation Building" in the Kennedy Era* (Chapel Hill: University of North Carolina Press, 2000), and *The Right Kind of Revolution: Modernization, Development, and U.S. Foreign Policy from the Cold War to the Present* (Ithaca: Cornell University Press, 2010); Nils Gilman, *Mandarins of the Future: Modernization Theory in Cold War America* (Baltimore: Johns Hopkins University Press, 2007).

14. *Next Generation*—"Who Watches the Watchers" 1989.

15. Adam Kotsko, *Neoliberalism's Demons: On the Political Theology of Late Capital* (Stanford: Stanford University Press, 2018).

SIX

Star Trek and the Marxist Theory of the State

The broadcast iterations of the *Star Trek* franchise present a future where human society is classless and free of ethnic, gender biases (chapter 1). While *Star Trek* casts the future of humanity as inherently egalitarian and fundamentally fair, other species (societies) are depicted as repressive and authoritarian. Therefore, the *Star Trek* text offers a (fictional) comparative analysis of states within these starkly different circumstances. *Star Trek* indicates that societies based on *federation* (liberal humanism) are rather immune to corruption and authoritarianism among their political elites because of the success of whistle-blowing—since such societies and their elites (overall) are committed to truth and honesty. In contrast, oppressive and repressive states in *Star Trek* are directly linked to embedded, caste-like elites (entrenched class hierarchy and hegemony).

In this latter case dominant elites are a class in-themselves, for-themselves (as Marx put it). Put differently, they prioritize their own power over the needs and well-being of society as a whole—violently suppressing any perceived challenge to their authority.[1] This view of elites is most sharply evident in the leadership group of the Dominion (featured in *Deep Space Nine*), known as the Founders. Nonetheless, contemporary capitalist elites are also suggested in *Star Trek* to act/think as a class in-themselves, for themselves (à la the Founders).

I begin the analysis by treating the state and politics within the Federation—where the governing norms are fairness and equality. The overall analysis and conclusion offered in this chapter is ostensibly consonant with Marx's view that a repressive modern state apparatus is directly, solely a function of class hegemony and oppression.

GOVERNANCE WITHIN MODERNITY

While humanity in *Star Trek* has ostensibly embraced values and economics envisioned by Karl Marx, the state in *Star Trek* has seemingly not withered away. Quite the contrary, the state appears as more entrenched than ever—with Starfleet (the military institution of the Federation)—at the center of the franchise. But are Starfleet and the Federation state institutions? There is the question in the writings of Marx of what exactly is meant by the state.[2] No doubt Marx believed that the state as the ultimate enforcer of class stratified capitalist society would be discarded along with capitalism.

Star Trek indicates that government and governance institutions would be required in advanced modernity. After all, how can society construct huge, immensely complicated spaceships in the absence of governance? How can a fleet of such starships be effectively deployed without a coordinating, commanding institution (Starfleet)? Additionally, how can the principles of universal justice and fairness inherent in Marxism be upheld across interstellar space without a government to normalize and uphold them (the Federation)? Hence, *Star Trek* suggests that Marx and Marxism do not predict anarchy/anarchism.[3]

How can citizens be certain that government and governance institutions aren't actually states (intended to repress) or will not become states over the course of time? Naeem Inayatullah in his essay "Bumpy Space: Imperialism and Resistance in *Star Trek: The Next Generation*"[4] seeks to link the Federation's mission to "seek out new life and new civilizations" with imperialism. In the episode "First Contact" (1991) the Chancellor of Malcor, upon first learning of the Federation and meeting Captain Picard, points out that "my world's history has recorded that conquerors often arrive with the words, 'We are your friends.'" Picard explains that "trust takes time and experience"—an ostensibly sensible response. Nevertheless, Inayatullah rather cynically holds that "Picard's answer obfuscates the critical issue: the hidden desires that lie beneath the apparently benevolent intentions of the Federation."[5] Why would Inayatuallah suggest that the Federation would have "hidden desires"? Inayatullah expressly conflates the Federation with Western imperialism: "In Western life, not much thought has gone into the desires and intentions of missionaries."[6] After expressly likening the American and British imperial projects to the Federation, Inayatullah writes "the dominance of the teaching drive over the need to learn sustains the usual props for benevolent imperialism."[7]

Inayatullah asks "why engage" the Malcorians and other societies on the verge of discovering warp speed—a velocity faster than light.[8] Inayatullah rejects the idea that helping a society into the fraternity of warp-capable societies is necessary to harmonize relations between polities with such advanced capabilities—the reasoning offered by Picard. Instead, Inayatullah holds that Picard is murky in explaining why the Federation seeks to "guide" the Malcorians. Inayatullah appears intent on the idea that the only reason a power like that of the Federation would be interested in new peoples is imperialism—i.e., resource exploitation and political hegemony. (Inayatuallah doesn't ask if the purpose of the Federation in "contacting" the Malcorians is motivated by imperial/hegemonic designs, why wait until the Malcorians are on the verge of warp speed capabilities?)

One point I make in *The Politics of* Star Trek is how shockingly (or willfully) ignorant of the *Star Trek* text its critics are.[9] Arguably the most anti-imperialist episode ever on American television is the original series episode "Mirror, Mirror" (1967)—treated above. "Mirror, Mirror" opens with a discussion between Kirk and the leader of the "Halkans" (named "Tharn"). The Halkans refuse to allow the Federation to mine the dilithium crystals on their planet because "dilithium crystals represent awesome power. Wrongful use of that power, even to the extent of the taking of one life, would violate our history of total peace." Kirk asks "When may we resume discussion?" Tharn: "The council will meditate further, but do not be hopeful of any change." Tharn adds: "Captain, you do have the might to force the crystals from us, of course." Kirk: "But we won't." While in the Federation universe the *Enterprise* only pursues peaceful means with the Halkans, in the Empire universe Kirk is "ordered to annihilate the Halkans unless they comply. *No alternative*." Kirk (from the Federation universe) incurs great risks in an effort to prevent the destruction of the Halkans. "Mirror, Mirror" is an explicit rejection/critique of military intervention into other societies—particularly for purposes of controlling natural resources.

On the question of imperialism or hegemony with regard to the Federation, the episode "The Paradise Syndrome" (1968) is also noteworthy. The *Enterprise* crew comes upon a group of Native American tribes transported to an alien planet. ("A mixture of Navajo, Mohican, and Delaware, I believe. All among the more advanced and peaceful tribes.") Significantly, no effort whatsoever is made to colonize or interfere with the transported natives. Instead, Kirk et al. succeeds in ensuring that the tribes can continue their premodern existence undisturbed.

In the (*Next Generation*) episode "Time's Arrow" (1992) Samuel Clemens (aka Mark Twain) (transported to the twenty-fourth century) assumes that the Federation represents/institutes a regime of conquest and control. His reasoning is based on the existence of the starship *Enterprise* i.e., the political/economic regime he thinks it represents. "Huge starships, and weapons that can no doubt destroy entire cities, and military conquest as a way of life?" One factor that proves Clemens wrong about the *Enterprise* and the Federation is the technology it does not employ—the "cloaking device." The cloaking device is introduced in the original series, and it is a weapon deployed/developed by the Romulan Empire. Later, the Klingon Empire adopts this technology as well. It allows star ships to travel under a shield ("cloak") of invisibility. The cloaking device is a tremendous tactical weapon—as ships can approach enemies totally undetected, thereby allowing devastating surprise attacks. A Romulan commander tells of a battle where Klingon "warships decloaked, they took us completely by surprise. The Klingons managed to destroy half my squadron before we even opened fire" (*Next Generation*—"Face of the Enemy" 1993). Glaringly and significantly, when a Starfleet officer surreptitiously develops cloaking technology for the Federation his actions (once discovered) are denounced as criminal and expressly in violation of the law: "As Captain of the *Enterprise*, I'm placing you under arrest" (*Next Generation*—"The *Pegasus*" 1994). Notably, the United States pioneered the development/use of stealth military airplanes—designed to evade enemy radar and, hence, execute surprise aerial attacks.[10] Another stealth technology pioneered by the United States is "predator drones,"[11] where operators in an air-conditioned facility in Nevada guide small airplanes (drones) flying over remote regions of the world, and with the push of a button fire missiles on unsuspecting individuals from fifty thousand feet.[12]

The fact that the Federation foregoes cloaking/stealth technology communicates that its starships—to the extent that they have military capabilities—are deployed solely for purposes of defense. Cloaking/stealth military technology is expressly offensive in nature—solely intended for the vanquishing of enemies, including rebellions. The fact that Federation ships do not have this offensive capability serves to substantiate the claim that the *Enterprise* "is a ship of peace. Not of war" (*Next Generation*—"Yesterday's *Enterprise*" 1990).

THE THREAT OF ELITES

The *Star Trek* text does address the concern that the governance institutions of Starfleet and the Federation can become *states*. The franchise does issue a specific warning about elites and their potential corruption and power hunger—even in the context of Federation. In the *Deep Space Nine* episode "Homefront" (1996) a terrorist bombing occurs on Earth—killing twenty-seven. In the aftermath of this attack, Starfleet (i.e., the military) argues for greater security measures. The president of Earth resists this suggestion: "I understand the need for increased security, but . . ."

> **President**: I believe the changeling threat is somewhat less serious than Starfleet does.
>
> **Admiral Leyton**: Mister President, I assure you the threat is real.
>
> **President**: For all we know, there was only one changeling on Earth, and he may not even be here anymore.

Captain Sisko: But if he is here, we have a problem. There's no telling how much damage one changeling could do.

President: Forgive me for saying so, Captain, but you sound a little . . . paranoid

Sisko: Do I?

This exchange presages the Bush administration contention that the Al-Qaeda threat required greater political/legal latitude for the military-security apparatus.[13] President Bush took this position even though the 9/11 attack involved only a handful of perpetrators, many of whom died in the attack.

In the end, the Earth president agrees to the enhanced security measures being proposed by the military. Interestingly, the enhanced security measures are seemingly instituted with simply the president's signature—there are no other deliberations presented or discussed.

These increased security measures are cast as necessary defensive measures to protect "paradise" or utopia (i.e., Earth):

President: I would hate to be remembered as the Federation President who destroyed paradise.

Sisko: We're not looking to destroy paradise, Mister President. We're looking to save it.

Just like the Bush administration would later argue for enhanced security measures and greater power for the presidency to protect "our American way of life."[14]

In the denouement of "Homefront" Earth experiences a planetary-wide blackout. A state of emergency has been declared. The subsequent *Deep Space Nine* episode "Paradise Lost" (1996) begins by showing platoons of troops patrolling the street, and everyone submitting to security screening (blood tests)—to establish that they are not enemies. We learn that the power outage was perpetrated by elements within Starfleet. Thus, *Deep Space Nine* issues a caution against the use of national security threats to suspend civil and political rights, as well as democratic decision-making processes: "What you're trying to do is seize control of Earth and place it under military rule." "If that's what it takes to stop the Dominion."

In 2002 as the neoconservative agenda (i.e., invading Iraq) is gaining momentum both through the Bush government and the national media—most prominently the *New York Times*[15]—the *Enterprise* episode "Fallen Hero" aired. The *Enterprise* picks up the Vulcan Ambassador to the planet of Mazar—she has been recalled by her government. Soon after *Enterprise* departs, the Mazar government demands that the Vulcan ambassador (V'lar) return—sending ships in pursuit. After initially refusing to tell Captain Archer the cause of the current controversy, V'lar relents and informs the captain why the Mazarites are so eager for her return.

> The Mazarites pursuing us are criminals. They are members of an organization that's infiltrated all levels of government, making themselves wealthy and powerful at the expense of many innocent victims. Their methods include eliminating anyone who stands in their way.

She adds that "the corruption ran deeper than I thought."

Star Trek takes the optimist stance that in the context of *Federation*, the public can ultimately trust its leaders because whistle-blowing is inevitable and overall the governing elite can be counted on to do what's right. The *Next Generation* episode "Conspiracy" (1988) posits a scenario where aliens take over the bodies of the highest governing officials within Starfleet for a seemingly nefarious purpose. The alien takeover is stopped by officers within Starfleet who become suspicious of the behavior, decisions of the top commanders invaded by the aliens. (The aliens are killed before we learn the content of their plan.) Similarly, when Captain Sisko in the *Deep Space Nine* episode "Paradise Lost" (1996) comes to understand that his commanding officer is conspiring against the government of Earth, Sisko, along other officers subordinate to the conspirator, reject the chain of command and thwart the conspiracy. Additionally, when the crew of the Federation starship "Pegasus" (episode title) realized that their captain was engaging in illegal research into cloaking technology, they mutinied. Moreover, in the movie *Insurrection* (1998), once Picard et al. from the *Enterprise* learn that the Federation leadership has sanctioned the forced removal of a village they directly block this removal. Also, in the 2013 *Star Trek* movie *Into Darkness*, when the *Enterprise* crew learn that elements within Starfleet conducted a false-flag operation to initiate a war with the Klingons, Kirk et al. successfully expose the subterfuge. Therefore, the embedded institutional commitment to (or ethics of) *truth* (morality, legality, fairness) in Starfleet (Federation institutions) serves as an effective prophylactic to conspiracies to bamboozle the public—see below. As Picard informed Data: "Starfleet doesn't want officers who will blindly follow orders without analyzing the situation" (*Next Generation*—"Redemption" 1991).

Star Trek makes the claim that a prime duty of military officers' (political leaders') within *federation* is to prevent authoritarian outcomes. The *Deep Space Nine* episode "Past Tense" (1995) features the following exchange:

> Are humans really any different than Cardassians . . . or Romulans? If push came to shove, if something disastrous happened to the Federation, and we got frightened enough, or desperate enough, how would we react? Would we stay true to our ideals . . . or would we just [resort to authoritarian/oppressive means]?

Captain Sisko responds "I don't know. But as a Starfleet officer, it's my job to make sure we never have to find out."

The politics and government responses to whistle-blowing conveyed in *Star Trek* is starkly different to those politics and government responses in the United States.[16] Well-known government whistle-blowers Edward Snowden and Chelsea Manning have been aggressively persecuted, forced into exile (Snowden) and imprisoned (Manning) by the American government. Julian Assange, who facilitates whistle-blowing through Wikileaks, has been similarly persecuted.[17]

Star Trek presumes a commitment to the truth among the military/political leaders of *Federation* to ensure that the institutions of governance are not used to establish a state. This is in sharp contrast to the leaders of *empire*. In pursuing the invasion of Cardassia and thereby ending the decades-old Klingon-Federation alliance, the Klingon Empire head of government, Chancellor Gowron, declares that "history is written by the victors" (*Deep Space Nine*—"The Way of the Warrior" 1995). Contrary to this sentiment that the perception of reality (facts) is malleable and can/should be shaped to serve any (corrupt) agenda, Captain Picard declares that "The first duty of every Starfleet officer is to the *truth*. Whether it's scientific truth, or historical truth, or personal truth. *It is the guiding principle upon which Starfleet is based*" (*Next Generation*—"The First Duty" 1992). In another instance, Picard, speaking to one of the leading political figures of the Federation ("Sarek"—episode title 1992), declares: "Sarek of Vulcan never confused what he wanted with the *truth*" (*Next Generation*).

This (fictional) commitment to the truth among Federation elites is in sharp contrast to the George W. Bush administration use of the weapons of mass destruction (WMD) hoax to induce an invasion of Iraq. The Downing Street Memo is a case in point. The memo written by a high-ranking British government official offered the opinion that the Bush administration was seeking to "fix the facts around the policy" in pushing for the invasion of Iraq.[18] Ron Suskind in 2004 described the following encounter with a Bush administration aide (presumed to be Karl Rove):

> The aide said that guys like me were "in what we call the reality-based community," which he defined as people who "believe that solutions emerge from your judicious study of discernible reality." . . . "That's not the way the world really works anymore," he continued. "We're an empire now, and when we act, we create our own reality. And while you're studying that reality—judiciously, as you will—we'll act again, creating other new realities, which you can study too, and that's how things will sort out. We're history's actors . . . and you, all of you, will be left to just study what we do."[19]

More succintly, *history is written by the victors* (i.e., the American empire).[20]

Star Trek offers templates and signposts to distinguish between a government and a state.

The franchise, however, goes further in positing an argument with regard to elites that are entrenched via class. *Star Trek* indicates that such elites conceptualize themselves as ruling castes, and they actively oppose any effort that challenges their dominance and/or authority. As I explain below, this conclusion has significant implications for Marxist state theory. For it indicates that entrenched hegemonic elites exercise direct control of the state, and do not solely hold power over the state through indirect means.

RULING CASTES

The clearest case of a ruling caste in *Star Trek* is the Founders of the Dominion. But prior to the Dominion, *Star Trek* the original series offered a lucid example of a ruling caste in the episode "The Cloud Minders" (1969). As noted earlier, this episode depicts a society (the planet of Ardana) where torture technology ("the rays")—and unsurprisingly racism—are used to maintain/stabilize a caste system.

When Kirk explains to the leader of Ardana that a simple filter-mask would protect the Troglytes from the negative effects of a gas in the zenite mines, and this would allow them to reach their full intellectual potential as well as allow them to fully integrate into Stratos' society, the leader angrily forbids Kirk from interfering in Ardana's affairs. Later, Ardana's leader complains that Captain Kirk "knows nothing except how to destroy our power."

A great deal of *Deep Space Nine* (which aired in the 1990s) revolves around the Dominion and the Federation/Klingon/Romulan war against it. The Dominion (from the Gamma Quadrant) is a violent empire populated by genetically engineered and mass produced technicians (Vorta) and soldiers (Jemh'dar) who are totally subservient to the Founders. During season 5 the Dominion invades the Alpha Quadrant intent on conquering the Federation (along with all of the quadrant) and "eradicating" the Earth's population.[21]

The leadership caste of the Dominion—the Founders—is composed of a species that mostly live in a liquid state. As noted above, the leadership caste of Ardana is not concerned about justice but only about power and maintaining order. The same is true of the Founders. They justify their empire through the idea that "many years ago we set ourselves the task of imposing order on a chaotic universe." As a species the Founders are known as "Changelings," and one changeling tells another (named Odo—who was separated from the Founders): "It's not justice you desire, Odo, but order. The same as we do" (*Deep Space Nine*—"The Search" 1994).

The Founders (who oversee a massive military) are cast as ruthless and place no value whatsoever on the lives of individuals outside of their caste. In one noteworthy scene a Founder decides that a new set of Vorta humanoids should be brought in to research a cure for the affliction she is suffering from. The Founder is informed a "team of Vorta Doctors [is] working night and day to find a cure." The Founder orders: "have them document their efforts. *Then eliminate them*." "Founder?" her Vorta aide asks. She explains "activate their clones and order them to continue their predecessors' work. Perhaps a fresh perspective will speed matters along."[22]

The Dominion has politically absorbed Cardassia, and rebels mobilize against Dominion rule. At the first sign of disobedience among the Cardassian populace, the Founder in charge orders the destruction of a Cardassian city as collective punishment—killing "two million." Ultimately, the Founder orders the destruction of all of Cardassia's cities.[23] In 2003 the American government wantonly and illegally invaded the country of Iraq, subsequently killing untold numbers and leveling entire cities.[24]

The science fiction notion that the callousness of American governing elites can be attributable to their being an alien species (a biologically distinct caste) is posited in the 1988 movie *They Live*. The corporate and political elite are (hideous looking) aliens overseeing a heartless neoliberal global economy/regime. The aliens' identities are masked by a machine that allows them to look like humans.

The extreme concentration of wealth characteristic of the neoliberal world system is indicative of extreme concentrations of political authority, whereby the "billionaire class" does constitute an entrenched class, caste that is socially and politically alienated from the rest of society.[25] The wealth and income of the economic elite (billionaire class) allow it to accumulate superior (seemingly insuperable) amounts of other valuable resources, such as social status,[26] deference,[27] publicity,[28] prestige,[29] organization,[30] campaign finance,[31] lobbying,[32] political access,[33] and legal[34] and scientific expertise.[35]

This has profound implications for the long-running debate among Marxist scholars over the nature and content of the state within capitalist society.[36] One strand of thinking among Marxist scholars holds the argument (dating to the 1970s) that political elites (elected and appointed public officials) are not directly subservient to capitalist elites, but are nevertheless hostage to the ideological structures and imperatives embedded with the capitalist, free market system.[37] The present configuration of wealth and political authority, however, strongly indicates that capitalist elites exercise direct control of the state apparatus (à la the Dominion).[38]

AMERICAN CAPITALIST ELITES IN *STAR TREK*

The *Star Trek* franchise depicts American capitalist elites as indifferent to the suffering of others, self-important, and prioritizing their own well-being above that of others. The *Deep Space Nine* episode "Past Tense" doesn't depict capitalist elites as nonhuman, but, nevertheless, capitalists are portrayed as an overly privileged caste—inured to the suffering and desperation of the masses. The creators of the episode juxtapose the poverty and destitution of the residents of "Sanctuary Districts" (where the poor and dispossessed of 2024 America are forcibly interned) with the life of opulence of the economic elites. After conveying/treating the dismal conditions that inhere in the Sanctuary District of San Francisco, the next scene (somewhat jarringly) is of a party of impeccably dressed and manicured well-to-do discussing their large-scale business projects and vacations: "I hear you just came back from Christchurch?" . . . "Yes. Did a little skiing on Mount Cook." . . . "You're lucky. We had to cancel our trip to the Alps this year because of the student protests in France." While, again, these elites are not aliens, they do seemingly think of the poor as a different species: Sanctuary Districts "keep *those people* off the streets." Another capitalist elite deludes himself into thinking the districts are for the benefit of its residents: "That's the whole point of the Sanctuary. To give people in trouble food and a place to stay." A social critic observes: "If that's all it's for, then why is there a wall around it?"

In "The Neutral Zone" (*Next Generation*—1988) (referred to above) the twentieth-century capitalist, Ralph Offenhouse, is completely self-absorbed. Upon being awoken from his cryogenic slumber, he explains that "I have a substantial portfolio. It's critical I check on it." Later, he adds "I have to phone Geneva right away about my accounts. The interest alone could be enough to buy even this ship." Ralph dons an attitude of arrogance, entitlement, and authority. He tells Captain Picard "I demand you see me." When Picard tries to put Ralph off by referring to the sensitive situation the ship is dealing with at the time, Ralph retorts "I'm sure that whatever it is seems very important to you. My situation is far more critical." Ralph condescends the Captain: "It is simply that I have more to protect than a man in your position could possibly imagine. No offense, but a military career has never been considered upwardly mobile."

"Future's End" (*Star Trek: Voyager*) takes place in the late twentieth-century—the year 1996 (when the episode aired). The action of this episode centers on Henry Starling. By the time that *Voyager* comes into contact with Starling he is a very wealthy technology wizard, like Steve Jobs and Bill Gates. ("Our Mister Starling has built himself quite a corporate empire. Looks like he's got wealth, celebrity and an ego to match.") Starling is only able to introduce "breakthrough" technologies to the twentieth-century because years earlier in 1967 he came upon a space ship from the future. Over time Starling was able to pilfer technology from the ship.

Voyager's mission in "Future's End" is to discover why a ship from 1996 sought to travel in time, thereby destroying Earth's solar system in the twenty-ninth-century. We learn that it will be Starling that will destroy the solar system when he tries to go to the twenty-ninth-century to retrieve more "new" technology for his commercial ventures. He is no longer able to extract usable technology from the ship he found years earlier. ("I've cannibalized the ship itself as much as I can. There's nothing left to base a commercial product on.")

Janeway warns Starling that his attempt to travel into the future will lead to massive catastrophe. Starling, nevertheless, is determined to pursue his goal. Janeway rebukes Starling for his lack of ethics: "You'd destroy an entire city? [Starling threatens to destroy present-day Los Angeles if Janeway tries to stop him.] You don't care about the future, you don't care about the present. Does anything matter to you, Mister Starling?" Starling feels justified in his means and the risk he is creating because his goal is "The betterment of mankind." More specifically, he is driven by technological advancement (at least for his time period):

> **Starling**: My products benefit the entire world. Without me there would be no laptops, no internet, no barcode readers. What's good for Chronowerx [Starling's company] is good for everybody. I can't stop now. One trip to the twenty-ninth century and I can bring back enough technology to start the next ten computer revolutions.
>
> **Janeway**: In my time, Mister Starling, no human being would dream of endangering the future to gain advantage in the present.

In response, Starling openly dismisses the devastation that could (will likely) result from his actions: "Captain, the future you're talking about, that's nine hundred years from now. I can't be concerned about that right now. I have a company to run and a whole world full of people waiting for me to make their lives a little bit better."

One cannot help but think of the fact that U.S. capitalists (particularly in the energy sector) overtly oppose regulating greenhouse gas emissions, in spite of the escalating global devastation being brought about by climate change.[39] Corporate leaders in the U.S. energy sector seemingly adopt Starling's amazingly callous stance with regard to global warming: "Global warming is about the future, we can't be concerned about that right now. We have companies to run and a whole world full of people waiting for us to make their lives a little bit better."[40]

CONCLUSION

The *Star Trek* franchise provides important insight into the post-capitalist conception of society that inheres in Marxist theory. While the state may wither away in a classless world (as predicted by Marx), *Star Trek* indicates that governance and government will persist. Such governance and government is necessary to oversee a technologically advanced modernity and to normalize and uphold the universal justice foreseen (hoped for) by Marx. While Starfleet and the Federation represent governance and government, they are not states (repressive, oppressive institutions). This is particularly indicated by the technology that the Federation and Starfleet forego and legally ban (e.g., cloak technologies). *Star Trek* goes further: the values that shape the Federation and Starfleet makes corruption and authoritarianism a virtual impossibility—as these institutions are deeply imbued with the values of honesty and truth. In such an environment, whistle-blowing is a virtual certainty and such whistle-blowing will find a receptive audience among fellow elites.

The *Star Trek* franchise indicates that an authoritarian state is directly linked and the result of an entrenched elite or class—that conceptualizes itself as a ruling caste. Such a state is the means through which a caste maintains its power and dominant social position. Such a caste and state are not concerned with justice, truth, or the well-being of others, society, but only with their power. This is consistent with a particular Marxist view of the capitalist state. Perhaps more significantly, a state is directly a product of entrenched elites that conceptualize themselves as a hegemonic caste. This suggests that in a just society—free of entrenched privileged classes and of gender, ethnic biases—humanity need not fear the formation of a state.

NOTES

1. Edward Andrew, "Class in Itself and Class against Capital: Karl Marx and His Classifiers," *Canadian Journal of Political Science* 16, no. 3 (1983): 577–84.
2. Solomon F. Bloom, "The 'Withering Away' of the State," *Journal of the History of Ideas* 7, no. 1 (1946): 113–21; Clyde W. Barrow, *Critical Theories of the State* (Madison: University of Wisconsin Press, 1993).
3. Colin Ward, *Anarchism: A Very Short Introduction* (New York: Oxford University Press, 2004); Leslie Holmes, *Communism: A Very Short Introduction* (New York: Oxford University Press, 2009).
4. Naeem Inayatullah, "Bumpy Space: Imperialism and Resistance in *Star Trek: The Next Generation*," in *To Seek Out New Worlds: Science Fiction and World Politics*, Jutta Weldes, ed. (New York: Palgrave Macmillan, 2003).
5. Ibid., 55.
6. Ibid., 54.
7. Ibid., 58.
8. Ibid., 55.
9. George A. Gonzalez, *The Politics of* Star Trek*: Justice, War, and the Future* (New York: Palgrave Macmillan, 2015).
10. Jack David, *B-2 Stealth Bombers* (New York: Torque Books, 2007); Christopher Drew, "Costliest Jet, Years in Making, Sees the Enemy: Budget Cuts," *New York Times*, November 29, 2012, A1.
11. Adam B. Schiff, U.S. House of Representatives member (who serves on the House Permanent Select Committee on Intelligence), noted in 2014 that "The United

States is the only country with a significant armed drone capability." Adam B. Schiff, "Let the Military Run Drone Warfare," *New York Times*, March 13, 2014, A27. Also see: Joe Cochrane, "At Asia Air Show, Plenty of Competition for Sales of Drones," *New York Times*, February 17, 2014, B2.

12. John F. Burns, "U.N. Panel to Assess Drone Use," *New York Times*, January 25, 2013, A4; Lloyd C. Gardner, *Killing Machine: The American Presidency in the Age of Drone Warfare* (New York: New Press, 2013); Thom Shanker, "Simple, Low-Cost Drones a Boost for U.S. Military," *New York Times*, January 25, 2013, A12; Declan Walsh, and Ihsanullan Tipu Mehsud, "Civilian Deaths in Drone Strikes Cited in Report," *New York Times*, October 22, 2013, A1; Christine Sixta Rinehard, *Drones and Targeted Killing in the Middle East and Africa: An Appraisal of American Counterterrorism Policies* (Lanham, MD: Rowman & Littlefield, 2016); Charlie Savage, "Order Limits Report of Deaths from U.S. Airstrikes," *New York Times*, March 7, 2019, A14.

13. Ryan J. Barilleaux and Christopher S. Kelley, eds., *The Unitary Executive and the Modern Presidency* (College Station: Texas A&M University Press, 2010).

14. "After the Attacks: Bush's Remarks to Cabinet and Advisers," *New York Times*, September 13, 2001. Web; Barilleaux and Kelley, *The Unitary Executive and the Modern Presidency*.

15. Don Van Natta, Jr., Adam Liptak, and Clifford J. Levy, "The Miller Case: A Notebook, a Cause, a Jail Cell and a Deal," *New York Times*, October 16, 2005, sec. 1, p. 1.

16. David McCraw, "Where Leaks and the Law Meet," *New York Times*, September 4, 2017, A2.

17. Geoffroy de Lagasnerie, *The Art of Revolt: Snowden, Assange, Manning* (Stanford: Stanford University Press, 2017); Liam Stack, "Manning Freed From Jail, But She May Return Soon," *New York Times*, May 10, 2019, A14; Charlie Savage, "Assange Indicted Over Leak as U.S. Expands Charges," *New York Times*, May 24, 2019, A1.

18. Terry H. Anderson, *Bush's Wars* (New York: Oxford University Press, 2011), 102.

19. Ron Suskind, "Faith, Certainty and the Presidency of George W. Bush," *New York Times Magazine*, October 17, 2004. Web.

20. Daniel H. Nexon and Thomas Wright, "What's at Stake in the American Empire Debate," *American Political Science Review* 101, no. 2 (2007): 253–71.

21. The Vorta (Weyoun) in charge of the Dominion war effort opines that after its victory the Dominion should "eradicate" the Earth's "population" to prevent any "organized resistence" (*Deep Space Nine*—"Sacrifice of Angels" 1997).

22. *Deep Space Nine*—"Penumbra" 1999.

23. *Deep Space Nine*—"What You Leave Behind" 1999.

24. Michael R. Gordon and Bernard E. Trainor, *Cobra II: The Inside Story of the Invasion and Occupation of Iraq* (New York: Vintage, 2007); Thomas E. Ricks, *Fiasco: The American Military Adventure in Iraq, 2003 to 2005* (New York: Penguin, 2007).

25. Clyde W. Barrow, *Critical Theories of the State* (Madison: University of Wisconsin Press, 1993), 17; Barrow explains that "corporations emerged as the dominant economic institutions in capitalist societies by the end of the nineteenth century." He goes on to note that as early as the late 1920s "the bulk of U.S. economic activity, whether measured in terms of assets, profits, employment, investment, market shares, or research and development, was concentrated in the fifty largest financial institutions and five hundred largest nonfinancial corporations." Ibid. Also see, Thomas Piketty, *Capital in the Twenty-First Century*, trans. Arthur Goldhammer (Cambridge, MA: Belknap Press, 2014); Patricia Cohen, "Study Finds Global Wealth Is Flowing to the Richest," *New York Times*, January 19, 2015, B6; Gerry Mullany, "World's 8 Richest Have as Much Wealth as Bottom Half, Oxfam Says," *New York Times*, January 16, 2017. Web.

Political Scientists Jeffrey A. Winters and Benjamin I. Page, writing in 2009, hold that "it is now appropriate to . . . think about the possibility of *extreme* political inequality, involving great political influence by a very small number of extremely wealthy individuals." They go on to add that "we argue that it is useful to think about the U.S. political system in terms of oligarchy." Jeffrey A. Winters and Benjamin I.

Page, "Oligarchy in the United States," *Perspectives on Politics* vol. 7, no. 4 (2009): 744, emphasis in original; also see Paul Krugman, "Oligarchy, American Style," *New York Times*, November 4, 2011, A31, and "The Undeserving Rich," *New York Times*, January 20, 2014, A17; Jeffrey A. Winters, *Oligarchy* (New York: Cambridge University Press, 2011); Shaila Dewan and Robert Gebeloff, "One Percent, Many Variations," *New York Times*, January 15, 2012, A1; David Leonhardt, "All for the 1%, 1% for All," *New York Times*, May 4, 2014, MM23; Nicholas Kristof, "An Idiot's Guide to Inequality," *New York Times*, July 24, 2014, A27; Anna Bernasek, "The Typical Household, Now Worth a Third Less," *New York Times*, July 27, 2014, BU6; Neil Irwin, "Economic Expansion for Everyone? Not Anymore," *New York Times*, September 27, 2014, B1; Robert Frank, "Another Widening Gap: The Haves vs. the Have-Mores," *New York Times*, November 16, 2014, BU4; Peter Eavis, "It's Never Been Easier to Be a C.E.O., and the Pay Keeps Rising," *New York Times*, May 26, 2019, BU4.

26. Paul Krugman, "Paranoia of the Plutocrats," *New York Times*, January 27, 2014, A19.

27. Nicholas Confessore, "Big-Money Donors Demand Larger Say in Party Strategy," *New York Times*, March 2, 2014, A1.

28. Carl Hulse and Ashley Parker, "Koch Group, Spending Freely, Hones Attack on Government," *New York Times*, March 21, 2014, A1.

29. Gail Collins, "Billion Dollar Babies," *New York Times*, March 6, 2014, A29.

30. Gordon Lafer, *The One Percent Solution: How Corporations Are Remaking America One State at a Time* (Ithaca, NY: Cornell University Press, 2017).

31. Timothy Kuhner, *Capitalism v. Democracy: Money in Politics and the Free Market Constitution* (Palo Alto: Stanford University Press, 2014); Robert E. Mutch, *Buying the Vote: A History of Campaign Finance Reform* (New York: Oxford University Press, 2014); John Attanasio, *Politics and Capital: Auctioning the American Dream* (New York: Oxford University Press, 2018); Shane Goldmacher and Jonathan Martin, "Democrats Rely on Rich Backers but Keep It Quiet," *New York Times*, March 31, 2019, A1.

32. Zephyr Teachout, *Corruption in America: From Benjamin Franklin's Snuff Box to Citizens United* (Cambridge, MA: Harvard University Press, 2014); Robert Pear, "Eager to Sink Medicare Plan, Lobbies Unite," *New York Times*, February 24, 2019, A1.

33. Eric Lipton, "(Legal) Sprees With Lobbyists," *New York Times*, January 20, 2014, A1, and "Energy and Regulators on One Team," *New York Times*, December 7, 2014, A1; Tara Siegel Bernard, "A Citizen's Guide to Buying Political Access," *New York Times*, November 19, 2014, F7; Carl Hulse, "Is the Supreme Court Naïve about Corruption? Ask Jack Abramoff," *New York Times*, July 6, 2016, A15; Robert Pear, "Trump Administration's Plea to Health Care Industry Surprises Experts," *New York Times*, November 25, 2018, A20.

34. Joshua Barkan, *Corporate Sovereignty: Law and Government Under Capitalism* (Minneapolis: University of Minnesota Press, 2013); Eric L. Lewis, "Who Are 'We the People'?" *New York Times*, October 5, 2014, SR1.

35. Barrow, *Critical Theories of the State*, 16; Nicholas Confessore, "Public Goals, Private Interests in Debt Campaign," *New York Times*, January 10, 2013, A1; Eric Lipton, "Fight Over Wage Illustrates Web of Industry Ties," *New York Times*, February 10, 2014, A1; Eric Lipton, Nicholas Confessore, and Brooke Williams, "Top Scholars or Lobbyists? Often It's Both," *New York Times*, August 9, 2016, A1.

36. Clyde W. Barrow, *Toward a Critical Theory of States: The Poulantzas-Miliband Debate After Globalization* (Albany: State University of New York Press, 2016).

37. Manuel Castells, *The Information Age: Economy, Society, and Culture*, vols. 1–3 (Malden, MA: Blackwell, 1996/1998); Susan Strange, *The Retreat of the State: The Diffusion of Power in the World Economy* (New York: Cambridge University Press, 1996); William Greider, *One World, Ready or Not: The Manic Logic of Global Capitalism* (New York: Simon & Schuster, 1997); Kees Van der Pijl, *Transnational Classes and International Relations* (New York: Routledge, 1998); Michael Hardt and Antonio Negri, *Empire* (Cambridge, MA: Harvard University Press, 2000); Alan Tonelson, *The Race to the Bottom: Why a Worldwide Worker Surplus and Uncontrolled Free Trade are Sinking*

American Living Standards (Boulder, CO: Westview, 2000); Leslie Sklair, *The Transnational Capitalist Class* (Malden, MA: Blackwell, 2001), and *Globalization: Capitalism and Its Alternatives* (New York: Oxford University Press, 2002); William I. Robinson, *A Theory of Global Capitalism: Production, Class, and State in a Transnational World* (Baltimore: Johns Hopkins University Press, 2004), and *Latin America and Global Capitalism: A Critical Globalization Perspective* (Baltimore: Johns Hopkins University Press, 2010).

38. Ralph Miliband, *The State in Capitalist Society* (New York: Basic Books, 1969); Barrow, *Critical Theories of the State*, chap. 1; George A. Gonzalez, *Corporate Power and the Environment* (Lanham, MD: Rowman & Littlefield, 2001), *The Politics of Air Pollution* (Albany: State University of New York, 2005), and *Energy, the Modern State, and the American World System* (Albany: State University of New York Press, 2018); G. William Domhoff, *Who Rules America?*, 7th ed. (New York: McGraw-Hill, 2013); Alex Hertel-Fernandez, *State Capture: How Conservative Activists, Big Businesses, and Wealthy Donors Reshaped the American States and the Nation* (New York: Oxford University Press, 2019).

39. George A. Gonzalez, *Energy and Empire: The Politics of Nuclear and Solar Power in the United States* (Albany: State University of New York Press, 2012), and *American Empire and the Canadian Oil Sands* (New York: Palgrave Macmillan, 2016).

40. For instance, Lisa Friedman, "How a Coal Baron's Wish List Became Trump's To-Do List," *New York Times*, January 10, 2018, B1.

SEVEN

Art as Liberation

Theodor W. Adorno controversially held that the fine arts (paintings, sculpture, classical music), within oppressive (capitalist) circumstances, can be a respite for the repressed masses. Adorno's specific argument is that fine art can serve as a counterweight to the homogenization, literal sameness, of modernity—vis-à-vis mass production and heavily commercialized (mostly lowbrow[1]) popular entertainment.[2] The *Star Trek* text offers three distinct critiques of the idea of fine art being politically useful to the masses in the context of oppression and extreme class stratification. First, dominant groups deny fine art to the masses. This argument is clearly evident in the original series episode "Cloud Minders" (1969). Second, art and beauty (of all sorts) can be the subject of an unhealthy fixation. Adorno seems to be promoting such a pathology. Third, the fine arts are only a source of liberation from the repetition of modernity within a broad context of freedom and justice. *Star Trek* conveys a utopian (modernist) society that is classless and completely free of ethnic, gender biases. The fine arts are not something that are only appreciated by all, but practiced by all. This is part of a full, rich life. More broadly, the fine arts are central to the advancement of humanity as a whole.

"THE CLOUD MINDERS"

In this episode the *Enterprise* crew visit the world of Ardana—a Federation member—in order to retrieve a mineral (zenite) vitally needed to combat a disease that catastrophically threatens all plant life of another Federation planet. Kirk et al. gets drawn into the civil strife of Ardana, as a rebellion by the laboring class known as Troglytes is blocking the delivery of the much-needed zenite. We learn that Ardana is sharply stratified—with the Troglytes living on the barren surface, and the governing caste living in the splendor of Stratos (a city literally floating in the clouds). Significantly, the prime output of Stratos is art ("art is the population's chief occupation")—something that Kirk and Spock initially admire ("I hear its art forms are incomparable"). They quickly, however, come to see that the life dedicated to the high arts of Stratos dwellers is directly predicated on the political, economic subjugation of the Troglytes—who spend their lives toiling in the zenite mines (Spock: "Those who receive the rewards are totally separated from those who shoulder the burdens").

"Cloud Minders" is a metaphor of how the professionalized fine arts are almost completely dominated by the rich. The museums that Adorno celebrates as oases of intellectual freedom are organized, financed, and led by wealthy elites.[3] What kind of art would be produced by residents of Stratos?—who expressly use hateful racism ("Troglytes are not like Stratos dwellers. . . . They're a conglomerate of inferior species"). It is safe to presume that the subject matter that dominates Stratos art would not be that which would draw in the Troglytes—their daily lives, their communities, their meager possessions, their families, etc. Therefore, the physical separation of Stratos (a city of the fine arts in the sky) from the Troglytes (the laboring class toiling in mines) is symbolic of the separation of the capitalist-dominated (professionalized) fine arts from the kinds of fine art that would intuitively arouse the interests of the working class.[4]

Importantly, the Stratos government expressly seeks to keep Troglytes ignorant and even intellectually stunted. The *Enterprise*'s Doctor McCoy comes to discover that there is a gas in the zenite mines that is mentally and psychologically impairing the Troglytes. When Captain Kirk offers the leader of Ardana an inexpensive filter that would allow the Troglytes to reach their full potential and to achieve their subsequent integration into Stratos society, the leader of Ardana sternly rejects Kirk's efforts at social reform. At one point he orders Kirk's death, complaining that Kirk "knows nothing except how to destroy our power and our society."

The Stratos leadership actively conspiring against the Troglytes' intellectual capabilities is a metaphor of how workers are kept ignorant of the fine arts. Art appreciation is something that is gained by being informed of the arguments and motifs that permeate and surround fine art.[5] Adornos's argument,[6] for instance, of fine art being a much-needed antidote to the forces of standardization and conformity within modernity is central to appreciating the kind of art that is evident on Stratos—art based entirely on form and color (Figure 7.1) and excluding social, political commentary, or observation. Even in the advanced world there has been an unrelenting assault on fine arts education.[7]

The *Star Trek* text indicates that the denial of art is among the most profound forms of oppression. This argument is evident with the Borg—who indiscriminately conquer and absorb worlds. The Borg (first appear-

Figure 7.1. The Art of Stratos. *Star Trek*.

ing in *The Next Generation*) embraces technology to such an extreme extent that they replace large parts of their body (and brain) with gadgets. (Every Borg is mechanically altered—by force if necessary.) The Borg are described as "a mixture of organic and artificial life." They inform their victims that "resistance is futile. Your life as it has been is over." "We will add your biological and technological distinctiveness to our own. Your culture will adapt to service ours." Among the Borg, individuality is erased: "You are not dealing with an individual mind. . . . It is the collective minds of all of them" (*Next Generation*—"Q Who" 1989).

The Borg travel in grayish giant cubes, and inside these lit cubes there are no signs of recreation; creativity; or family life. The straight lines, precise right angles and dark hues inside the Borg ships bespeak extreme utilitarianism, a perfectly efficient, rationalist use of space and color—bereft of anything that could be distracting; or that makes life worth living (*Next Generation*—"Who Q" and "Best of Both Worlds" 1990). Borg are referred to as "drones" and their social organization is labeled a "hive" (*Voyager*—"Drone" 1998). Arguably, most damning of all the Borg cannot create knowledge, only assimilate it (i.e., appropriate it from others).[8]

ART AS UNHEALTHY FIXATION

Star Trek also indicates that a turn to art and beauty in a context of social dysfunction (as advised by Adorno) can itself be a pathology. In the *Next Generation* episode "Hollow Pursuits" (1990) a crew member of the *Enterprise* has social phobias and turns to the "Holodeck"—a device that allows people to create three-dimensional narratives and fantasies—to assuage his anxieties and interpersonal frustrations. His continuing social difficulties results in a greater and greater retreat from the actual world and into the "art" of the Holodeck.

The original series episode "The Way to Eden" (1969) involves a group trying to escape what it perceives as the oppression of modern life and is seeking the planet "Eden"—a bucolic world where the biosphere is not manipulated/affected by the technology of the twenty-third century. ("It is almost a biological rebellion. A profound revulsion against the planned communities, the programming, the sterilized, artfully balanced atmospheres. They hunger for an Eden where spring comes.") The group is cast as violently pursuing its goal—hijacking the *Enterprise* and attempting to kill the crew. In the end, the planet they identify as Eden (while beautiful) contains vegetation and plant-life that is entirely toxic and poisonous. With this disappointment, the leader of the group commits suicide. The seeming point is an obsessive fixation on the beauty of nature (or art) is evidence of an unstable mental state. An inference one could make from the episode "Hollow Pursuits."

At the core of *Star Trek* text is the argument that societal liberation, justice is precisely about allowing everyone to engage in art—the arts of science, discovery, as well as the humanities. This liberation is achieved through the Marxist progressive dialectic.

LIBERATION AND CREATIVITY

As indicated in chapter 1, the turn from capitalism allowed for society's focus to shift squarely upon the "enrichment" or "betterment" of humankind—as Captain Picard in "Neutral Zone" and Jake Sisko in "In the Cards" put it. What does this enrichment or betterment mean in practice? It seemingly does involve the fine arts, as particularly in the *Next Generation* crew members are depicted playing classical music, painting, and participating in plays. Captain Picard in two distinct instances is shown serving as mentor to Lt. Cmd. Data as Data acts out scenes from Shakespeare (*Henry V*) ("The Defector" 1990) and Dickens (*A Christmas Carol*) ("Devil's Due" 1991). Thus the fine arts are not something to be appreciated by those fortunate enough to have access to museums, music halls, or playhouses, but personally engaging in the fine arts is something that is part of a well-rounded life for everyone. Captain Janeway of *Voyager* critiques the idea of art as a profession when she observes that artistic "tastes change" ("Virtuoso" 2000).

But the fine arts serve a broader purpose in the *Star Trek* text. *Star Trek* indicates the purpose of humanity is precisely to *speculate* about the world/universe through both science and the humanities.

THE ADVANCEMENT OF HUMANITY

Why do the humans in *Star Trek* venture into deep space?—to enrich and better humanity. Thus, exploring space, finding new worlds, ideas, cultures is part of the effort (along with the fine arts) to enhance the life of humans as well as to advance humans (collectively).

Human society as a whole is *intellectually growing, emotionally maturing* (i.e., becoming more rational) in *Star Trek*. Gene Roddenberry created the *Star Trek* franchise and was the prime creative force behind the original series as well as the animated series (1973–1974) that followed. Toward the end of his life Roddenberry gave an extended interview where he did indicate that the totality of human history is a progressive telos (dialectic) (à la Marx). Roddenberry labeled humanity's telos a "socio-organism":

> The usual way of the physical world is to progress towards unity. When life originated on this planet, it was a single-cell organism. And perhaps by accident, or need for survival, or some primal urge, these individual cells began to group together to form collectives, then units, then a corporate body. And that's what happens on a larger scale with humans. They form groups—tribes, nations, and so on. . . . If you follow the thought logically, you can project a more complex interaction—perhaps a thinking body in which the individual units no longer function in any capacity as individuals. They may specialize, but not without the knowledge and cooperation of the whole group. It's a kind of interdependence in which the whole is greater than the sum of its part.[9]

Roddenberry pointed to "computers" (science, technology) as an advancement toward human unity—drawing people together through increased information and communication flows. Thus, the original series was very optimistic about computers, even as they were a nascent technology in the late 1960s (when *Star Trek* was produced).[10]

Interestingly, in the *Star Trek* franchise the evolving rationality, maturity of humanity is referred to most explicitly in the animated series. The episode "The Magicks of Megas-Tu" (1973) invokes the Salem witch trials. Old world "devils, warlocks, evil sorcerers" were the misunderstood, maligned, massacred aliens (Megans) that the *Enterprise* was now encountering. The Megans now fearful of humans, place Kirk et al. on trial: "These are the defendants, as representatives of the vilest species in all the universe, treacherous humanity." In humanity's defense Kirk explains: "in the centuries since the Salem witch trials we have learned. We try to understand and respect all life forms. . . . The records of the *Enterprise* are open for your inspection. All the history of Earth and the Federation is at your disposal." In an effort to tap into the prejudices of humans, the *Enterprise* crew is told that the one Megan that has befriended, protected them is no less than "the Rollicker, the Tempter, Lucifer" himself. Kirk, reflecting modern, secular, humane reasoning, retorts: "We're not interested in legend. He's a living being, and intelligent life form. That's all we have to know about him. We will not join in harming him." The Megans decide to imprison Lucifer for eternity for aiding the *Enterprise*. Kirk risks death to protect, help Lucifer: "I have to, or you'll become as bad as the Earthmen you fear. You're acting out of terror instead of out of thought or respect." This convinces the aliens that humans have indeed evolved: "The Megans had to have proof that mankind had grown and learned wisdom since they last saw Earth. Your compassion was that proof, Captain."

"The Eye of the Beholder" (1974) is an episode where Kirk et al. end up as specimens in the zoo of a highly advanced species. Ultimately, Kirk's captors conclude that the *Enterprise* crew doesn't belong in a zoo because humans "are considered simplistic, but in the process of evolving into a higher order." Spock (who can engage in telepathic communication with the aliens) goes on to explain "it seems they were where we are some tens of thousands of centuries ago." Similarly, in the episode "Bem" (1974) an advanced alien creature recognizes that humans have evolved in terms of rationality and intellect: (to Kirk et al.)

> Punishment? What is punishment? Revenge? Intelligent beings need no revenge. Punishment is necessary only where learning cannot occur without it. You are behind that. My children here [a primitive peoples the entity oversees] are not. That is why you must leave, so as not to corrupt their development with concepts that they are not yet ready for.

The dichotomy between ancient people and modern humanity is again referenced in "How Sharper Than a Serpent's Tooth"[11] (1974). A powerful creature (Kukulkan) that visited Earth thousands of years ago is again visiting Earth and demanding the deference (worship) that he received from primitive humans: "You are my children. I hoped I could teach you, help you." Kirk: "You did, long ago, when it was needed most. Our people were children then. Kukulkan, we've grown up now. We don't need you anymore." Realizing the validity of Kirk's argument, Kukulkan, deflated: "I will let you go your own way. I have already done what I can."

CONCLUSION

Theodor Adorno argues that the fine arts can be liberating within the context of modern capitalism. The *Star Trek* text offers a different view of art. The original series episode "The Clouder Minders" is an explicit metaphor of how the masses in a class stratified society are actively denied fine art—both because the content of said art is not directed at the broad public and because fine arts education tends to be the domain of the well-to-do. Additionally, using art (beauty) as an escape (as advocated by Adorno) can be a manifestation of mental instability. This argument is articulated in the *Next Generation* episode "Hollow Pursuits" and the original series episode "This Way to Eden."

More generally, in the *Star Trek* franchise art can only serve as liberating in a context of social liberation—where humanity is freed from the drive toward capital accumulation (i.e., capitalism, neoliberalism). In such a context the arts are not only appreciated by the public but practiced by all. The humanities are at the core of humanity's intellectual and emotional advancement—along with science and space exploration.

NOTES

1. Lawrence Levine, *Highbrow/Lowbrow: The Emergence of Cultural Hierarchy in America* (Cambridge, MA: Harvard University Press, 1990).

2. Martin Morris, *Rethinking the Communicative Turn: Adorno, Habermas, and the Problem of Communicative Freedom* (Albany: State University of New York Press, 2001); Michael Feola, *The Powers of Sensibility: Aesthetic Politics through Adorno, Foucault, and Ranciere* (Evanston: Northwestern University Press, 2018).

3. Andrea Fraser, *2016: In Museums, Money, and Politics* (Cambridge, MA: MIT Press, 2018); Ginia Bellafante, "The Shed as Dispensation from Capital Sin," *New York Times*, April 7, 2019, MB3.

4. Tony Bennett, *The Birth of the Museum: History, Theory, Politics* (New York: Routledge, 1995); Timothy W. Luke, *Museum Politics: Power Plays at the Exhibition* (Minneapolis: University of Minnesota Press, 2002).

5. Peter Brooks, ed., *The Humanities and Public Life* (New York: Fordham University Press, 2010).

6. Theodor W. Adorno, *Aesthetic Theory* (Minneapolis: University of Minnesota Press, 1998 [1970]).

7. James Davison Hunter, *Culture Wars: The Struggle to Control the Family, Art, Education, Law, and Politics In America* (New York: Basic Books, 1992); Andrew Hartman, *A War for the Soul of America: A History of the Culture Wars* (Chicago: University of Chicago Press, 2015).

8. "The Borg gain knowledge through assimilation. What they can't assimilate, they can't understand" (*Voyager*—"Scorpion" 1997).

9. Yvonne Fern, *Gene Roddenberry: The Last Conversation* (Los Angeles: University of California Press, 1994), 16.

10. Ibid., 46.

11. This is also a quote from *King Lear*.

Conclusion

A Future Only If There Is Justice

In *The Politics of* Star Trek, writing in 2015, I hold that the *Star Trek* franchise allows us to compare Cold War politics with post–Cold War politics.[1] This is because the creators of *Star Trek* have been writing and speculating about politics for over fifty years. The *Star Trek* franchise began in the late 1960s during a time when New Deal and Great Society politics predominated, and the alternative was Soviet "socialism." Later *Star Trek* begins in the late 1980s and runs until 2005. During 2017 the franchise was restarted with the series *Discovery*. Beginning in the 1980s with the onset of the Reagan Revolution, and the subsequent collapse of the Soviet Union (circa 1990), what occurs is a decisive turn against the social justice politics that predominated in the late 1960s and toward the global trend of free market capitalism (i.e., neoliberalism). The result is more turbulent international relations,[2] the use of torture, drone assassination, and in the present period the return of white supremacy (racism) as a salient aspect of statecraft (as reflected in *Discovery*).

The *Star Trek* franchise, however, does more than reflect, depict the political currents of the times—as significant as this is. The *Star Trek* text also presents an argument as to what constitutes a just, stable, and thriving society. Such a society is predicated on the *progressive dialectic*—resulting in a modern world, free of class cleavages, and gender and ethnic biases. This dialectic is consonant with the notions of revolutionary change and progress postulated by Karl Marx.[3] *Star Trek,* along with other popular culture venues, also provides insight into whether the current neoliberalist world system is a dystopia (chapter 3).

THE OPTIMISM OF THE LATE 1960S VERSUS THE PESSIMISM OF THE PRESENT

Elsewhere I draw a comparison between the original series episode "Cloud Minders" (1969) and the *Star Trek: Voyager* episode "Alliances" (1996).[4] Both episodes invoke race relations in the developing world. The template for each episode is seemingly South Africa. In "Cloud Minders" Kirk et al. visits the Federation member planet of Ardana—where the mining of "zenite" is the prime economic activity. The dramatic tension in the episode is centered on a Troglyte resistence movement that is preventing the *Enterprise* from completing its mission of transporting zenite from Ardana to another planet in desperate of it (needed to save its plant life). Captain Kirk in the end is able to broker an agreement between the Troglytes and the Stratos dwellers.

The episode "Alliances" similarly depicts ethnic tensions. In this instance, the fair-skinned Trabe exploited and brutalized the dark-skinned Kazons (who sport dreadlocks). Eventually, the Kazons rose up and forced the Trabe to flee their planet and live as space-faring nomads when the *Voyager* crew comes upon them. Janeway seeks to broker a peace deal between the Trabe and the Kazons, but she is unable to do so—as the hostility between the two is too deep and intense.

What is theoretically and historically significant is that the optimism of "Cloud Minders" is rooted in the fact that the Troglytes are offered social justice to end their rebellion. A "filter" will prevent them from suffering the cognitively impairing effects of mining zenite, and this will allow them to be effectively integrated into Stratos society. Hence, technology and state power (in the form of the *Enterprise* crew) are deployed to forward universal prosperity and establish social peace. In sharp contrast, all Janeway can offer the Kazon to stop harassing the Trabe is the promise of "stability." Therefore, in the context of neoliberalism (systemic privatization) social justice is implicitly off the agenda and the result is continuing strife and violence.

The *Star Trek* franchise offers another cross-generational comparison with the original series episode "City on the Edge of Forever" (1967) and the *Star Trek: Deep Space Nine* episode "Past Tense" (1995). "City on the Edge of Forever" is predominately set in Depression era New York City. Kirk and Spock return to the past to correct history. When they transport to Depression era New York City Kirk and Spock immediately witness the poverty of the period. Strongly indicative of the idea that such societal-wide poverty and despair are things of the past, Kirk says, "I've seen old photographs of this period. An economic upheaval had occurred." Spock remarks, "It was called Depression, circa 1930. Quite barbaric." Seemingly reflective of the optimism of the New Deal and the Great Society of the late 1960s, one Edith Keeler makes the following speech to a room of homeless in the midst of the Depression:

> I don't pretend to tell you how to find happiness and love when every day is just a struggle to survive, but I do insist that you do survive because the days and the years ahead are worth living for. One day soon man is going to be able to harness incredible energies, maybe even the atom. Energies that could ultimately hurl us to other worlds in some sort of spaceship. And the men that reach out into space will be able to find ways to feed the hungry millions of the world and to cure their diseases. They will be able to find a way to give each man hope

> and a common future, and those are the days worth living for. Our deserts will bloom.

Again, science, technology, and public policy (i.e., modernity) are optimistically viewed as forwarding universal prosperity.[5] Arguably, this optimism helped fuel the American war effort that would defeat the Nazis—as this victory was a central feature of the episode narrative.

"Past Tense" centers on the Bell Uprising—which, due to a historical accident, is led by Sisko. Residents of the Sanctuary District take hostages, and Sisko is demanding economic justice for all district residents: "We want the Sanctuaries closed and the Federal Employment Act reinstated." "All we're asking for is a chance to get back on our feet again. We don't deserve to be locked up in here." Another uprising leader indicates that this demand will never be met: "Why don't you have them throw in a couple of silk shirts, maybe a penthouse in Singapore. Jobs? You guys want jobs? When are you going to get it? There are no jobs. Not for us, anyway." In the end, this cynicism turns out to be accurate, as the state's only response is the threat of violence.

> **Public official**: The Governor assures me that if you let the hostages go, he'll reduce the charges against you to incitement to riot.
>
> **Webb**: That's it? What about closing the Sanctuary, what about jobs?
>
> **Public official**: The Governor intends to form a committee to look into the problems facing the District residents.
>
> **Sisko**: So what you're telling us is that nothing is going to change.
>
> **Public official**: Gentlemen, if I were you I would seriously consider taking this offer. . . The Governor is not going to let this situation continue forever.

In the final instance, it is the governor who demands the violent repression of the uprising: "Governor, I understand your concern, but I think the use of force would be premature at this time. . . . The Governor's made up his mind. We move in at oh five hundred."

Unlike "City on the Edge of Forever" where normal politics ostensibly results in social justice (the New Deal—with Franklin Roosevelt reverentially invoked), in "Past Tense" progressive social change only comes about through a violent uprising. The Bell Uprising is described as "one of the most violent civil disturbances in American history." "The government troops will storm this place" and the uprising "will change public opinion about the Sanctuaries. They'll be torn down and the United States will finally begin correcting the social problems it had struggled with."

REPRESSION NOT JUSTICE

In the absence of justice, elites will turn to repression to maintain stability (as is evident with the episode "Past Tense"). "Mirror, Mirror" (1967—original series) depicted a polity based on repression. Captain Jonathan Archer (*Star Trek: Enterprise*) from the alternative universe declares that "Great men are not peacemakers. Great men are conquerors" ("In a Mirror, Darkly" 2005). Communicating the political theory at the heart of the Empire: Spock explains that "Terror must be maintained or the Empire is doomed. It is the logic of history." Put differently, stability in the Empire is maintained through repression.

In the Empire (of "Mirror, Mirror" and later "In a Mirror, Darkly") torture technologies called an "agonizer" and an "agony chamber" exist. The agony chamber is also depicted in *Star Trek: Discovery* when the Discovery visits the Empire universe ("Vaulting Ambition" and "What's Past Is Prologue"—both 2018). When used they cause extreme pain without causing tissue damage. "In a Mirror, Darkly" the following is explained of the "agony booth": "Traditional forms of punishment can overwhelm the nervous system. After a time, the brain ceases to feel anything." "These sensors continually shift the stimulation from one nerve cluster to another, keeping the subject in a constant state of agony." Thus, pain can endlessly be inflicted. Such fictional technologies presage the 2003 Bush administration notorious memo authorizing torture. In this memo perpetual, intense pain was deemed legally allowable. Only "death, organ failure or permanent damage resulting in a loss of significant body functions will likely result" were prohibited.[6] While the Bush administration didn't develop infinite pain machines, i.e., agonizers or agony chambers, (as far as we know) technologies/practices like "water boarding" (where drowning is simulated) were used hundreds of times on individual victims.[7]

In "Mirror, Mirror" Kirk apprised Spock of a weapon ("the Tantalus field"). From one's quarters a person could zero in on victims and with the push of a button make them disappear (assassinate them). This presages U.S. drone technology, where operators in an air-conditioned facility in Nevada guide small airplanes (drones) flying over remote regions of the world, and with the push of a button fire missiles on unsuspecting individuals from 50,000 feet.[8]

RACISM AS OFFICIAL POLITICS

"Cloud Minders" depicts a society (the planet of Ardana) where racism is used to maintain/stabilize a caste system. U.S. President Donald J. Trump, similarly, has based his government on racism.

In contrast to poverty, torture, drone assassination, racism, etc., the *Star Trek* text depicts the progressive dialectic. Thus, the *Star Trek* franchise, more than documenting the increasing dysfunction and barbarity of global politics, casts an affirmative argument as to how to achieve a just, stable, and thriving society. This argument is predicated on the concepts of social change and progress posited by Karl Marx.

JUSTICE AND *STAR TREK*

Star Trek reflects and effectively conveys the shifting, changing politics of the last fifty years. The franchise in the late 1960s captures the optimism of the New Deal and Great Society through such noteworthy episodes as "Cloud Minders" and "City on the Edge of Forever." With "Cloud Minders" we see the belief that the progressive politics of the era can establish peace and stability among the developed and developing world. In "City on the Edge of Forever" even the worst victims of the Depression find solace and hope in the efforts of the Roosevelt government to progressively combat poverty and economic despair.

With the victory of the Reagan Revolution and global neoliberalism, *Star Trek* of the 1980s and 1990s conveys the pessimism and cynicism resulting from the worldwide abandonment of social justice politics. The episode "Alliances" indicates that "stability" without justice is not possible. "Past Tense" depicts a narrative where the state relies entirely on repression in response to manifestations of resistance to poverty and economic hardship. The *Star Trek* franchise has historically posited the idea that regimes that rely on repression to maintain stability utilize torture, assassination, and racism. The U.S. presidential administration of Donald J. Trump (2017–) is directly predicated on racism and hate. *Discovery* suggests that such governments are inherently pugnacious and warmongering.

By necessity all political art is to some degree derivative of the politics and societies of their times. Nonetheless, for aesthetics to qualify as political art (I contend) it must stand outside of the politics of its time, even as it comments on those politics. Political art (as opposed to art that is political [i.e., propaganda]) expands the field of politics to incorporate ideas/arguments outside of the "official" or those discourses deemed acceptable. Thus, political art conveys the politics of the times, but goes further in offering insights into the times and beyond.[9] *Star Trek* goes outside of *official* discourses with the *progressive dialectic*—the notion that at the core of the American Project is a revolutionary process that will result in a classless society, free of gender and ethnic biases. The *Star Trek* progressive dialectic is consonant with the ideation of Karl Marx (who, in turn, was inspired by Georg Hegel). Therefore, even as *Star Trek* conveys the pessimism, even the hateful racism, that has come to dominate officialdom, it maintains an unflinching optimism based on the belief that humanity (as a whole) can create a world founded on justice and fairness.

CONCLUSION

As I outlined in the Introduction, humanity is recklessly careening toward inevitable disaster—whether it be nuclear war, global warming, or mass extinction due to ecosystem destruction civilization is facing (manmade) catastrophe the likes of which have never been witnessed by humans. The only way to hope to avoid a planetary cataclysm is through justice—more specifically, *communism* as a concept of justice. Particularly in the West, and especially after the Cold War, democracy has been equated with justice. As neoliberalism has become predominant, democracy has lost its normative meaning and purpose. Democracy has been reduced to hollow procedures (elections) that do not serve as a political basis to prevent or reform the extreme concentration of wealth (the Billionaire Class) nor the extreme concentration of political power (the Unitary Executive). Additionally, democracy has not been a prophylactic against the xenophobia that became especially salient under the auspices of the Global War on Terror. This facilitated the installation of the xenophobe Donald Trump as U.S. president and the political rise of xenophobic elements and parties in Europe as well. As explained in the Introduction communism is focused on outcome. Thus, society and humanity must be totally committed to combating global warming, poverty, ecosystem destruction, and political and economic inequality—the profound lack of fairness and democracy. The productive forces of society must be geared toward these goals—no longer should we expect humanity to thrive as an indirect result of the capital accumulation process. The optimism that humanity can and will embrace communism (as justice) to pull civilization back from the edge of catastrophe is found in popular culture. The *Star Trek* franchise (the most popular franchise in television history) has been portraying for over fifty years a society (the Federation) that's directly and unambiguously committed to the enhancement of humanity.

An obstacle to justice is analytic philosophy. Analytic philosophers abandoned the topic of justice when they equated knowledge solely with the laws of physics. Justice is a function of the Hegelian *absolute*—which we speculate (learn) about through art. The justice (knowledge) of the absolute is evolving through the progressive dialectic—as depicted in the *Star Trek* franchise. Today, we see an analytic philosopher seeking to stigmatize the progressive dialectic (*progressive history*) by falsely and disingenuously invoking science (chapter 1). In the absence of a coherent, universal concept of justice the next political turn could be one toward xenophobia and warmongering (i.e., the Trump Turn) (chapter 2). The dystopian Trump Turn would seemingly be accompanied or paralleled by an identity (grievance) politics turn—one where ethnic groups are dangerously and permanently cleaved into different, competing entities (chapter 4). Another obstacle to justice is religious political reasoning (theocracy). A rights regime based on prophetic reasoning is its own threat to humanity, as such politics serves to intellectually stunt the public and society by implication—as reason, empiricism, and the absolute are replaced by religious prophecy and revelation. Moreover, a rights regime can exist in conjunction with (be a central component of) a repressive state—where rights are the carrot serving to attain the public's acquiescence in the face of oppression and brutality (chapter 5).

The creators of *Star Trek* speculate as to how a communist society would operate. Government would be deployed to realize the full potential of modernity and to oversee the justice regime. In the absence of an entrenched hegemonic elite, government need not be feared. Put differently, a repressive state will not be formed (chapter 6). Communism (as a concept of justice) is not only about allowing humanity/civilization to survive. It is about the thriving of the individual and society by implication. This thriving occurs in part through art—where everyone to some degree engages the arts as part of a fulfilling life. Art is part of the discovery and enrichment of humanity. In *Star Trek* this enrichment is predominantly conveyed through space exploration and "going where no man/one has gone before" (chapter 7). But before humanity can chart this course toward universal personal enrichment and unending discovery, society must be fully based on a foundation of justice.

NOTES

1. George A. Gonzalez, *The Politics of* Star Trek (New York: Palgrave Macmillan, 2015), conclusion.
2. Clyde Haberman, "'This Is Not a Drill': The Growing Threat of Nuclear Cataclysm," *New York Times*, May 14, 2018, A15.
3. Peter Singer, *Marx: A Very Short Introduction* (New York: Oxford University Press, 2001); Gareth Jones Stedman, *Karl Marx: Greatness and Illusion* (Cambridge, MA: Harvard University Press, 2016).
4. Gonzalez, *The Politics of* Star Trek, 180.
5. Kenneth J. Bindas, *Modernity and the Great Depression: The Transformation of American Society, 1930–1941* (Lawrence: University of Kansas Press, 2017).
6. As quoted in Mark Mazzetti, "'03 U.S. Memo Approved Harsh Interrogations," *New York Times*, April 2, 2008. Web.
7. Scott Shane, "Waterboarding Used 266 Times on 2 Suspects," *New York Times*, April 20, 2009, A1; Jonathan Hafetz, "Don't Execute Those We Tortured," *New York Times*, September 25, 2014, A31; Mark Mazzetti, "Panel Faults C.I.A. over Brutality Toward Terrorism Suspects," *New York Times*, December 10, 2014, A1; Carol Rosenberg, "In Guantánamo Trials, Wrestling with Airing Evidence on Torture," *New York Times*, April 6, 2019, A1.
8. John F. Burns, "U.N. Panel to Assess Drone Use," *New York Times*, January 25, 2013, A4; Lloyd C. Gardner, *Killing Machine: The American Presidency in the Age of Drone Warfare* (New York: New Press, 2013); Thom Shanker, "Simple, Low-Cost Drones a Boost for U.S. Military," *New York Times*, January 25, 2013, A12; Declan Walsh and

Ihsanullan Tipu Mehsud, "Civilian Deaths in Drone Strikes Cited in Report," *New York Times*, October 22, 2013, A1.

9. Jacques Rancière, *Aesthetics and Its Discontents*, trans. Steve Corcoran (Malden, MA: Polity, 2009).

Bibliography

Abi-Habib, Maria. "India's Military, Ailing and Poor, Nears Its Brink," *New York Times*, March 4, 2019, A1.

Achen, Christopher H. *Democracy for Realists: Why Elections Do Not Produce Responsive Government* (Princeton: Princeton University Press, 2017).

Adamczak, Bini. *Communism for Kids* (Cambridge, MA: MIT Press, 2017).

Adorno, Theodor W. *Aesthetic Theory* (Minneapolis: University of Minnesota Press, 1998 [1970]).

"After the Attacks: Bush's Remarks to Cabinet and Advisers," *New York Times*, September 13, 2001. Web.

Alderman, Liz. "Humans Wanted, But Robots Work," *New York Times*, April 17, 2018, B1.

Allingham, Michael. *Choice Theory: A Very Short Introduction* (New York: Oxford University Press, 2002).

Anderson, Terry H. *Bush's Wars* (New York: Oxford University Press, 2013).

Andrew, Edward. "Class in Itself and Class against Capital: Karl Marx and His Classifiers," *Canadian Journal of Political Science* 16, no. 3 (1983): 577–84.

Attanasio, John. *Politics and Capital: Auctioning the American Dream* (New York: Oxford University Press, 2018).

Bacon, Michael. *Richard Rorty: Pragmatism and Political Liberalism* (Lanham: Lexington Books, 2007).

———. *Pragmatism* (Cambridge: Polity, 2012).

Baker, Peter. "Trump's Insults End a Brief Civil Interlude," *New York Times*, December 8, 2018, A10.

———. "Trump Calls Emergency, Defying Congress," *New York Times*, February 16, 2019, A1.

Barilleaux, Ryan J., and Christopher S. Kelley, eds. *The Unitary Executive and the Modern Presidency* (College Station: Texas A&M University Press, 2010).

Barkan, Joshua. *Corporate Sovereignty: Law and Government Under Capitalism* (Minneapolis: University of Minnesota Press, 2013).

Barnosky, Anthony D. *Dodging Extinction: Power, Food, Money, and the Future of Life on Earth* (Berkeley: University of California Press, 2016).

Barrow, Clyde W. *Critical Theories of the State* (Madison: University of Wisconsin Press, 1993).

———. *Toward a Critical Theory of States: The Poulantzas-Miliband Debate After Globalization* (Albany: State University of New York Press, 2016).

Bellafante, Ginia. "The Shed as Dispensation from Capital Sin," *New York Times*, April 7, 2019.

Bendersky, Joseph W. *Carl Schmitt: Theorist for the Reich* (Princeton, NJ: Princeton University Press, 1983).

Bennett, Tony. *The Birth of the Museum: History, Theory, Politics* (New York: Routledge, 1995).

Bennhold, Katrin. "Veering to Germany's Political Extremes," *New York Times*, October 13, 2018, A4.

———. "German Far-Right Group: Neo-Nazis Rebranded," *New York Times*, December 28, 2018, A1.

Bernard, Tara Siegel. "A Citizen's Guide to Buying Political Access," *New York Times*, November 19, 2014, F7.

Bernardi, Daniel Leonard. Star Trek *and History: Race-ing toward a White Future* (New Brunswick, NJ: Rutgers University Press, 1998).
Bernasek, Anna. "The Typical Household, Now Worth a Third Less," *New York Times*, July 27, 2014, BU6.
Bindas, Kenneth J. *Modernity and the Great Depression: The Transformation of American Society, 1930–1941* (Lawrence: University of Kansas Press, 2017).
Bloom, Solomon F. "The 'Withering Away' of the State," *Journal of the History of Ideas* 7, no. 1 (1946): 113–21.
Blow, Charles. "An Imperial Presidency?" *New York Times*, May 13, 2019, A19.
Bowles, Nellie. "As Birthrates Fall, Fearing 'Replacement' on Far Right," *New York Times*, March 19, 2019, A8.
Bowman, Brady. *Hegel and the Metaphysics of Absolute Negativity* (Cambridge: Cambridge University Press, 2015).
Bradsher, Keith. "2 Possible Paths Emerge in China Trade War," *New York Times*, August 9, 2018, B1.
———. "Trade Wedge For China: Its Minerals," *New York Times*, May 24, 2019, B1.
Bradsher, Keith, and Ana Swanson. "China Digs In on Subsidies as Trade Deal Stalls," *New York Times*, May 13, 2019, B1.
———. "Rethinking China's Role as the World's Factory," *New York Times*, April 6, 2019, A1.
Brooks, Peter, ed. *The Humanities and Public Life* (New York: Forham University Press, 2010).
Brown, Kate. *Dispatches from Dystopia: Histories of Places Not Yet Forgotten* (Chicago: University of Chicago Press, 2015).
Burns, Alexander. "Pushing Someone Rich, Trump Offers Himself," *New York Times*, June 17, 2015, A16.
Burns, John F. "U.N. Panel to Assess Drone Use," *New York Times*, January 25, 2013, A4.
Bush, Billy. "Yes, Donald Trump, You Said That," *New York Times*, December 4, 2017, A21.
Cannon, James P. *The History of American Trotskyism: Report of a Participant* (New York: Pioneer Publishers, 1944).
Capaldi, Nicholas. *The Enlightenment Project in the Analytic Conversation* (Boston: Kluwer Academic Publishers, 1998).
Caplan, Jane. *Nazi Germany (Short Oxford History of Germany)* (New York: Oxford University Press, 2008).
Carrington, André M. *Speculative Blackness: The Future of Race in Science Fiction* (Minneapolis: University of Minnesota Press, 2016).
Carwardine, Richard, and Jay Sexton, eds. *The Global Lincoln* (New York: Oxford University Press, 2011).
Casselman, Ben. "Nashville Leaves the Pack Behind," *New York Times*, December 17, 2018, B1.
Castells, Manuel. *The Information Age: Economy, Society, and Culture*, vols. 1–3 (Malden, MA: Blackwell, 1996/1998).
Chesnais, François. *Finance Capital Today: Corporations and Banks in the Lasting Global Slump* (Chicago: Haymarket Books, 2018).
Chidester, Jeffrey L., and Paul Kengor, eds. *Reagan's Legacy in a World Transformed* (Cambridge, MA: Harvard University Press, 2015).
Childs, Peter. *Modernism*, 3rd ed. (New York: Routledge, 2016).
Cochrane, Emily. "A Passive Congress Enables Trump to Use Pulpit to Continue His Shutdown Chatter," *New York Times*, December 25, 2018, A15.
Cochrane, Joe. "At Asia Air Show, Plenty of Competition for Sales of Drones," *New York Times*, February 17, 2014, B2.
Cohen, Patricia. "Study Finds Global Wealth Is Flowing to the Richest," *New York Times*, January 19, 2015, B6.
Collins, Gail. "Billion Dollar Babies," *New York Times*, March 6, 2014, A29.

Collins, Jane L., and Victoria Mayer. *Both Hands Tied: Welfare Reform and the Race to the Bottom in the Low-Wage Labor Market* (Chicago: University of Chicago Press, 2010).

Confessore, Nicholas. "Public Goals, Private Interests in Debt Campaign," *New York Times*, January 10, 2013, A1.

———. "Big-Money Donors Demand Larger Say in Party Strategy," *New York Times*, March 2, 2014, A1.

Connor, Steven. "Doing without Art," *New Literary History* 42, no. 1: 53–69.

Coogan, Michael D., ed. *Eastern Religions: Hinduism, Buddism, Taoism, Confucianism, Shinto* (New York: Oxford University Press, 2005).

Cooper, Helene. "Defense Chief Plans to Use War Funds to Build Wall," *New York Times*, May 11, 2019, A16.

Corasaniti, Nick. "Democrats, Flush with Power, Try to Grab More," *New York Times*, December 14, 2018, A1.

Cottle, Michelle. "Where's Your Climate Plan, Mr. McConnell?," *New York Times*, March 27, 2019, A22.

Danisch, Robert. *Pragmatism, Democracy, and the Necessity of Rhetoric* (Columbia: University of South Carolina Press, 2007).

Davenport, Coral, and Lisa Friedman. "From Very Beginning, Broad Effort to Loosen the Rules on Pollution," *New York Times*, November 27, 2018, A12.

Davenport, Coral, and Mark Landler. "In Climate Fight, Trump Will Put Science on Trial," *New York Times*, May 28, 2019, A1.

Davey, Monica. "A Picture of Detroit Ruin, Street by Forlorn Street," *New York Times*, February 18, 2014, A1.

David, Jack. *B-2 Stealth Bombers* (New York: Torque Books, 2007).

Davis, Julie Hirschfeld. "Trump Rants on Unauthorized Migrants: 'These Aren't People, These Are Animals,'" *New York Times*, May 17, 2018, A13.

de Greef, Kimon, and Sewell Chan. "Setback for U.S. Is Feared as Africa Recoils at Trump Remark," *New York Times*, January 16, 2018, A8.

de Lagasnerie, Geoffroy. *The Art of Revolt: Snowden, Assange, Manning* (Stanford: Stanford University Press, 2017).

Deringer, William. *Calculated Values: Finance, Politics, and the Quantitative Age* (Cambridge, MA: Harvard University Press, 2018).

Desch, Michael C. *Cult of the Irrelevant: The Waning Influence of Social Science on National Security* (Princeton: Princeton University Press, 2019).

———. "How Political Science Became Irrelevant," *Chronicle of Higher Education*, February 27, 2019. Web.

Desmond, William. *Art and the Absolute: A Study of Hegel's Aesthetics* (Albany: State University of New York Press, 1986).

Dewan, Shaila, and Robert Gebeloff. "One Percent, Many Variations," *New York Times*, January 15, 2012, A1.

Domhoff, G. William. *Who Rules America?*, 7th ed. (New York: McGraw-Hill, 2013).

Downey, Liam. *Inequality, Democracy, and the Environment* (New York: New York University Press, 2015).

Drape, Joe."Bankruptcy for Ailing Detroit, but Prosperity for Its Teams," *New York Times*, October 14, 2013, A1.

Drew, Christopher. "Costliest Jet, Years in Making, Sees the Enemy: Budget Cuts," *New York Times*, November 29, 2012, A1.

Drury, Shadia B. *Leo Strauss and the American Right* (New York: St. Martin's Press, 1997).

Dudley, Will, ed. *Hegel and History* (Albany: State University of New York Press, 2009).

Duménil, Gérard, and Dominique Lévy. *Capital Resurgent: Roots of the Neoliberal Revolution*, trans. Derek Jeffers (Cambridge, MA: Harvard University Press, 2004).

Eavis, Peter. "It's Never Been Easier to Be a C.E.O., and the Pay Keeps Rising," *New York Times*, May 26, 2019, BU4.

Eberl, Jason T., and Kevin S. Decker, eds. Star Trek *and Philosophy: The Wrath of Kant* (Chicago: Open Court, 2008).

Ede, Siân. *Art and Science* (New York: I. B. Tauris, 2005).
Edmondson, Catie. "G.O.P. Scorns Judges' Rating by Bar Group," *New York Times*, December 12, 2018, A1.
Elshtain, Jean. *Just War Against Terror: The Burden of American Power In a Violent World* (New York: Basic Books, 2008).
Eriksson, Lina. *Rational Choice Theory: Potential and Limits* (New York: Palgrave, 2011).
Erlanger, Steven. "Is U.S. Foreign Policy Reverting the World to a Dark 'Jungle'?" *New York Times*, September 23, 2018, A8.
———. "Far Right Is Seen Making Inroads As Europe Votes," *New York Times*, May 27, 2019, A1.
Fandos, Nicholas, and Sharon LaFraniere. "Two Reports on Meddling: Choose Your Own Verdict," *New York Times*, April 28, 2018, A14.
Fausset, Richard. "Daring to Say No to Big Oil," *New York Times*, February 5, 2019, B1.
———. "In America's Heartland, the Voice of Hate Next Door," *New York Times*, November 26, 2017, A16.
Feenberg, Andrew. *Technosystem: The Social Life of Reason* (Cambridge, MA: Harvard University Press, 2017).
Feola, Michael. *The Powers of Sensibility: Aesthetic Politics through Adorno, Foucault, and Ranciere* (Evanston: Northwestern University Press, 2018).
Fern, Yvonne. *Gene Roddenberry: The Last Conversation* (Los Angeles: University of California Press, 1994).
Fields, A. Belden. *Trotskyism and Maoism: Theory and Practice in France and the United States* (New York: Praeger, 1988).
Forst, Rainer. *Contexts of Justice*, trans. John M. M. Farrell (Berkeley: University of California Press, 2002).
Frank, Adam. "Is a Climate Disaster Inevitable?" *New York Times*, January 18, 2015, SR6.
Frank, Robert. "Another Widening Gap: The Haves vs. the Have-Mores," *New York Times*, November 16, 2014, BU4.
Frankfurt, Harry G. *On Bullshit* (Princeton: Princeton University Press, 2005).
Franklin, H. Bruce. *Crash Course: From the Good War to the Forever War* (Newark: Rutgers University Press, 2018).
Fraser, Andrea. *2016: In Museums, Money, and Politics* (Cambridge, MA: MIT Press, 2018).
Friedman, Lisa. "How a Coal Baron's Wish List Became Trump's To-Do List," *New York Times*, January 10, 2018, B1.
———. "E.P.A. Will Ease Path to New Coal Plants," *New York Times*, December 5, 2018, B3.
———. "E.P.A.'s Reckoning Is a Rosier View of Air Pollution," *New York Times*, May 21, 2019, A1.
Fukuyama, Francis. "After Neoconservatism," *New York Times Magazine*, February 19, 2006, 62.
Gail, William B. "A New Dark Age Looms," *New York Times*, April 19, 2016, A27.
Gallagher, Kelly Sims. *China Shifts Gears: Automakers, Oil, Pollution, and Development* (Cambridge, MA: MIT Press, 2006).
Gallagher, Mary Elizabeth. *Contagious Capitalism: Globalization and the Politics of Labor in China* (Princeton: Princeton University Press, 2005).
Gardner, Lloyd C. *Killing Machine: The American Presidency in the Age of Drone Warfare* (New York: New Press, 2013).
Gillis, Justin. "Scientists Sound Alarm on Climate," *New York Times*, March 18, 2014, D1.
———. "Study Warns of a Perilous Climate Shift within Decades," *New York Times*, March 23, 2016, A11.
Gilman, Nils. *Mandarins of the Future: Modernization Theory in Cold War America* (Baltimore: Johns Hopkins University Press, 2007).

Glock, Hans-Johann. *What Is Analytic Philosophy?* (New York: Cambridge University Press, 2008).

Goldmacher, Shane, and Jonathan Martin. "Democrats Rely on Rich Backers but Keep It Quiet," *New York Times*, March 31, 2019, A1.

Goldstein, Dana. "A More Perfect Civics Lesson? 'Democracy' Itself Is Up for Debate," *New York Times*, April 8, 2019, A1.

Gonzalez, George A. *Corporate Power and the Environment* (Lanham, MD: Rowman & Littlefield, 2001).

———. *The Politics of Air Pollution* (Albany: State University of New York, 2005).

———. *Energy and Empire: The Politics of Nuclear and Solar Power in the United States* (Albany: State University of New York Press, 2012).

———. *The Politics of* Star Trek: *Justice, War, and the Future* (New York: Palgrave Macmillan, 2015).

———. *American Empire and the Canadian Oil Sands* (New York: Palgrave Macmillan, 2016).

———. *The Absolute and* Star Trek (New York: Palgrave Macmillan, 2017).

———. *Energy, the Modern State, and the American World System* (Albany: State University of New York Press, 2018).

———. Star Trek *and the Politics of Globalism* (New York: Palgrave Macmillan, 2018).

———. *Popular Culture as Art and Knowledge* (Lanham, MD: Lexington Books, 2019).

———. *Popular Culture and the Political Values of Neoliberalism* (Lanham, MD: Lexington Books, 2019).

Goodman, Peter S. "U.S. and Global Economies Slipping in Unison," *New York Times*, August 24, 2008, A1.

———. "Chief of W.T.O. Worries about Its Role as Peacekeeper as a Trade War Brews," *New York Times*, March 24, 2018, A9.

Gordon, Michael R., and Bernard E. Trainor. *Cobra II: The Inside Story of the Invasion and Occupation of Iraq* (New York: Vintage, 2007).

Gordon, Paul. *Art as the Absolute: Art's Relation to Metaphysics in Kant, Fichte, Schelling, Hegel, and Schopenhauer* (New York: Bloomsbury Academic, 2015).

Green, Donald, and Ian Shapiro. *Pathologies of Rational Choice Theory: A Critique of Applications in Political Science* (New Haven: Yale University Press, 1996).

Greider, William. *One World, Ready or Not: The Manic Logic of Global Capitalism* (New York: Simon & Schuster, 1997).

Greven, David. *Gender and Sexuality in* Star Trek: *Allegories of Desire in the Television Series and Films* (Jefferson, NC: MacFarland, 2009).

Gross, Neil. *Richard Rorty: The Making of an American Philosopher* (Chicago: University of Chicago Press, 2008).

Grynbaum, Michael M., and John Koblin. "TV Host 'Ashamed' of Lewd Chat with Trump," *New York Times*, October 8, 2016, A12.

Haberman, Clyde. "'This Is Not a Drill': The Growing Threat of Nuclear Cataclysm," *New York Times*, May 14, 2018, A15.

Hacker, Jacob S. "Strong Economy, Worried Americans," *New York Times*, May 22, 2019, A21.

———. *The Great Risk Shift: The New Economic Insecurity and the Decline of the American Dream*, 2nd ed. (New York: Oxford University Press, 2019).

Hafetz, Jonathan. "Don't Execute Those We Tortured," *New York Times*, September 25, 2014, A31.

Hampshire, Stuart. *Justice Is Conflict* (Princeton: Princeton University Press, 2000).

Hardt, Michael, and Antonio Negri. *Empire* (Cambridge, MA: Harvard University Press, 2000).

Hartman, Andrew. *A War for the Soul of America: A History of the Culture Wars* (Chicago: University of Chicago Press, 2015).

Harvey, David. *A Brief History of Neoliberalism* (New York: Oxford University Press, 2007).

———. *Seventeen Contradictions and the End of Capitalism* (New York: Oxford University Press, 2014).

———. *Marx, Capital, and the Madness of Economic Reason* (New York: Oxford University Press, 2017).

Haverty-Stacke, Donna T. *Trotskyists on Trial: Free Speech and Political Persecution Since the Age of FDR* (New York: New York University Press, 2016).

Herf, Jeffrey. *The Jewish Enemy: Nazi Propaganda during World War II and the Holocaust* (Cambridge, MA: Harvard University Press, 2008).

Herndon, Astead W. "'Witch Hunts' and 'Fake News': Trump Grievances Go Local," *New York Times*, March 17, 2019, A20.

Hertel-Fernandez, Alex. *State Capture: How Conservative Activists, Big Businesses, and Wealthy Donors Reshaped the American States—and the Nation* (New York: Oxford University Press, 2019).

Hickman, Larry A. *Pragmatism as Post-Modernism: Lessons from John Dewey* (New York: Fordham University Press, 2007).

Holmes, Leslie. *Communism: A Very Short Introduction* (New York: Oxford University Press, 2009).

Hook, Sidney. *Towards the Understanding of Karl Marx* (New York: John Day, 1933).

Horkheimer, Max. *Critique of Instrumental Reason*, trans. Matthew O'Connell (New York: Verso, 2013).

Houlgate, Stephen. *Hegel's "Phenomenology of Spirit": A Reader's Guide* (New York: Bloomsbury Academic, 2013).

Hulse, Carl. "Is the Supreme Court Naïve about Corruption? Ask Jack Abramoff," *New York Times*, July 6, 2016, A15.

Hulse, Carl, and Ashley Parker. "Koch Group, Spending Freely, Hones Attack on Government," *New York Times*, March 21, 2014, A1.

Hunter, James Davison. *Culture Wars: The Struggle to Control the Family, Art, Education, Law, and Politics in America* (New York: Basic Books, 1992).

Huntington, Samuel P. *The Clash of Civilizations and the Remaking of World Order* (New York: Simon & Schuster, 1996 [2011]).

Hurdle, Jon. "Philadelphia Forges Plan to Rebuild from Decay," *New York Times*, January 1, 2014, B1.

Inayatullah, Naeem. "Bumpy Space: Imperialism and Resistance in *Star Trek: The Next Generation*," in *To Seek Out New Worlds: Science Fiction and World Politics*, Jutta Weldes, ed. (New York: Palgrave Macmillan, 2003).

Irwin, Neil. "Economic Expansion for Everyone? Not Anymore," *New York Times*, September 27, 2014, B1.

Israel, Jonathan I. *Radical Enlightenment: Philosophy and the Making of Modernity, 1650–1750* (New York: Oxford University Press, 2001).

———. *Enlightenment Contested: Philosophy, Modernity, and the Emancipation of Man, 1670–1752* (New York: Oxford University Press, 2006)

———. *The Expanding Blaze: How the American Revolution Ignited the World, 1775–1848* (Princeton: Princeton University Press, 2017).

Johnson, Paul. *Socrates: A Man for Our Times* (New York: Penguin, 2012).

Jones, Daniel Stedman. *Masters of the Universe: Hayek, Friedman, and the Birth of Neoliberal Politics* (Princeton: Princeton University Press, 2012).

Jones, Gareth Stedman. *Karl Marx: Greatness and Illusion* (Cambridge: Cambridge University Press, 2016).

Juss, Satvinder S., ed. *Beyond Human Rights and the War on Terror* (New York: Routledge, 2018).

Kaminsky, Jack. *Hegel on Art: An Interpretation of Hegel's Aesthetics* (Albany: State University of New York Press, 1962).

Kanno-Youngs, Zolan. "Cyberwarfare Is Top Threat Facing U.S., Nielsen Says," *New York Times*, March 19, 2019, A17.

Kant, Immanuel. *Critique of Pure Reason*, trans. Max Muller (New York: Penguin, 2008 [1781]).

Kemp, Martin. *Seen | Unseen: Art, Science, and Intuition from Leonardo to the Hubble Telescope* (New York: Oxford University Press, 2006).

Kershaw, Ian. *Hitler, the Germans, and the Final Solution* (New Haven: Yale University Press, 2009).

———. *Hitler: A Biography* (New York: Norton, 2010).

Kett, Joseph F. *Merit: The History of a Founding Ideal from the American Revolution to the Twenty-First Century* (Ithaca: Cornell University Press, 2013).

Klein, Steven. "The New Science Wars: Radical Differences in the Humanities and Sciences Haven't Gone Away—They've Intensified," *Chronicle of Higher Education*, December 16, 2018. Web.

Koistinen, David. *Confronting Decline: The Political Economy of Deindustrialization in Twentieth-Century New England* (Gainesville: University Press of Florida, 2013).

Kolbert, Elizabeth. *The Sixth Extinction: An Unnatural History* (New York: Henry Holt, 2014).

Kotsko, Adam. *Neoliberalism's Demons: On the Political Theology of Late Capital* (Stanford University Press, 2018).

Kramer, Andrew E. "A Day after U.S. Leaves Nuclear Pact Russia Announces It Will Do the Same," *New York Times*, February 3, 2019, A7.

Kramer, Andrew E., and Megan Specia. "The Risks to Russia, China and Europe as the U.S. Scraps a Nuclear Deal," *New York Times*, February 2, 2019, A9.

Kreines, James. *Reason in the World: Hegel's Metaphysics and Its Philosophical Appeal* (New York: Oxford University Press, 2015).

Kristof, Nicholas. "An Idiot's Guide to Inequality," *New York Times*, July 24, 2014, A27.

Krugman, Paul. "Oligarchy, American Style," *New York Times*, November 4, 2011, A31.

———. "Robots and Robber Barons," *New York Times*, December 10, 2012, A27.

———. "The Undeserving Rich," *New York Times*, January 20, 2014, A17.

———. "Paranoia of the Plutocrats," *New York Times*, January 27, 2014, A19.

———. "The Depravity of Climate-Change Denial," *New York Times*, November 27, 2018, A22.

———. "The G.O.P. Goes Full Authoritarian," *New York Times*, December 11, 2018, A26.

———. "Conservatism's Monstrous Endgame," *New York Times*, December 18, 2018, A22.

Kuhner, Timothy. *Capitalism v. Democracy: Money in Politics and the Free Market Constitution* (Palo Alto: Stanford University Press, 2014).

Lafer, Gordon. *The One Percent Solution: How Corporations are Remaking America One State at a Time* (Ithaca: Cornell University Press, 2017).

Landler, Mark. "Trump Leaves U.S. and China on Tip of New Cold War," *New York Times*, September 20, 2018, A1.

Landler, Mark, and Edward Wong. "Bolton Vows Bigger U.S. Role in Africa, but Goal Is Countering China's Sway," *New York Times*, December 14, 2018, A11.

Lasswell, Harold D. *Politics: Who Gets What, When, How* (New York: McGraw-Hill, 1936).

Latham, Michael E. *Modernization as Ideology: American Social Science and "Nation Building" in the Kennedy Era* (Chapel Hill: University of North Carolina Press, 2000).

———. *The Right Kind of Revolution: Modernization, Development, and U.S. Foreign Policy from the Cold War to the Present* (Ithaca: Cornell University Press, 2010).

Lenin, V. I. *Imperialism: The Highest Stage of Capitalism* (New York: Pluto, 1996 [1917]).

Leonhardt, David. "All for the 1%, 1% for All," *New York Times*, May 4, 2014, MM23.

———. "We're Measuring the Economy All Wrong," *New York Times*, September 14, 2018. Web.

———. "When C.E.O.s Cared about America," *New York Times*, December 3, 2018, A27.

———. "Companies Behind a Power Grab," *New York Times*, December 10, 2018, A27.

———. "Trump Encourages Violence," *New York Times*, March 18, 2019, A23.

———. "A C.E.O. Scared for His Country," *New York Times*, April 1, 2019, A21.

Lepore, Jill. "Don't Let Nationalists Speak for the Nation," *New York Times*, May 26, 2019, SR3.
Levin, Dan. "Billionaire Roulette," *New York Times*, November 11, 2018, ST1.
———. "'Justice' Prevails: Dictionary Picks 2018 Word of the Year," *New York Times*, December 18, 2018, A15.
Levine, Lawrence. *Highbrow/Lowbrow: The Emergence of Cultural Hierarchy in America* (Cambridge, MA: Harvard University Press, 1990).
Levitsky, Steven, and Daniel Ziblatt. *How Democracies Die* (New York: Crown, 2018).
Lewis, Eric L. "Who Are 'We the People'?" *New York Times*, October 5, 2014, SR1.
Lipton, Eric. "(Legal) Sprees with Lobbyists," *New York Times*, January 20, 2014, A1.
———. "Fight Over Wage Illustrates Web of Industry Ties," *New York Times*, February 10, 2014, A1.
———. "Energy and Regulators on One Team," *New York Times*, December 7, 2014, A1.
———. "Interior Nominee Helped Quash Pesticide Report," *New York Times*, March 27, 2019, A1.
Lipton, Eric, Nicholas Confessore, and Brooke Williams. "Top Scholars or Lobbyists? Often It's Both," *New York Times*, August 9, 2016, A1.
Little, Daniel. *New Directions in the Philosophy of Social Science* (Lanham, MD: Rowman & Littlefield, 2016).
Londoño, Ernesto, and Lisa Friedman. "Brazil Backs Out of Holding Climate Change Meeting for U.N.," *New York Times*, November 29, 2018, A4.
Luke, Timothy W. *Museum Politics: Power Plays at The Exhibition* (Minneapolis: University of Minnesota Press, 2002).
Lustgarten, Abrahm. "Fuel to the Fire," *New York Times Magazine*, November 25, 2018, 42.
Maira, Sunaina Marr. *The 9/11 Generation: Youth, Rights, and Solidarity in the War on Terror* (New York: New York University Press, 2016).
Maker, William, ed. *Hegel and Aesthetics* (Albany: State University of New York Press, 2000).
Malachowski, Alan. *The New Pragmatism* (Montreal: McGill-Queen's University Press, 2010).
Malcolm, Noel, ed. *Thomas Hobbes: Leviathan* (New York: Oxford University Press, 2012 [1668]).
Markoff, John. "When Apple Was Homegrown," *New York Times*, December 17, 2018, B6.
Marx, Karl. *The Critique of the Gotha Programme* (London: Electric Book Co., 2001 [1875]). Web.
———. *On the Jewish Question*, 1844, http://www.marxists.org/archive/marx/ works/ 1844/ jewish-question/.
May, Todd. "Would Human Extinction Be a Tragedy?" *New York Times*, December 17, 2018. Web.
Mazzetti, Mark. "'03 U.S. Memo Approved Harsh Interrogations," *New York Times*, April 2, 2008. Web.
———. "Panel Faults C.I.A. Over Brutality toward Terrorism Suspects," *New York Times*, December 10, 2014, A1.
McCraw, David. "Where Leaks and the Law Meet," *New York Times*, September 4, 2017, A2.
McCumber, John. *Time in the Ditch: American Philosophy and the McCarthy Era* (Evansville: Northwestern University Press, 2001).
———. *The Philosophy Scare: The Politics of Reason in the Early Cold War* (Chicago: University of Chicago Press, 2016).
McIntyre, Lee. *Post-Truth* (Cambridge, MA: MIT Press, 2018).
McKee, Guin A. *The Problem of Jobs: Liberalism, Race, and Deindustrialization in Philadelphia* (Chicago: University of Chicago Press, 2009).

McPherson, James M. *Abraham Lincoln and the Second American Revolution* (New York: Oxford University Press, 1992).

Menand, Louis. *The Metaphysical Club* (New York: Farrar, Straus, and Giroux, 2001).

Meyer, Frederick W. *Narrative Politics: Stories and Collective Action* (New York: Oxford University Press, 2014).

Miliband, Ralph. *The State in Capitalist Society* (New York: Basic Books, 1969).

Miller, Carol Poh, and Robert Wheeler. *Cleveland: A Concise History* (Bloomington: Indiana University Press, 2009).

Miller, Claire Cain. "Smarter Robots Move Deeper Into Workplace," *New York Times*, December 16, 2014, A1.

———. "What's Really Killing Jobs? It's Automation, Not China," *New York Times*, December 22, 2016, A3.

Misak, Cheryl. *The American Pragmatists* (New York: Oxford University Press, 2015).

Montgomery, David, and Annie Karni. "President Lauds Curbs to Energy Regulations," *New York Times*, May 15, 2019, A16.

Morris, Martin. *Rethinking the Communicative Turn: Adorno, Habermas, and the Problem of Communicative Freedom* (Albany: State University of New York Press, 2001).

Mosley, Layna. *Global Capital and National Governments* (Cambridge: Cambridge University Press, 2003).

Mounk, Yascha. "How Political Science Gets Politics Wrong," *Chronicle of Higher Education*, October 30, 2016. Web.

Moye, David. "Donald Trump Appeared in a Playboy Softcore Porn Video," *Huffington Post*, September 30, 2016. Web.

Mullany, Gerry. "World's 8 Richest Have as Much Wealth as Bottom Half, Oxfam Says," *New York Times*, January 16, 2017. Web.

Mutch, Robert E. *Buying the Vote: A History of Campaign Finance Reform* (New York: Oxford University Press, 2014).

Myers, Constance Ashton. *The Prophet's Army: Trotskyists in America, 1928–1941* (Westport, CT: Greenwood Press, 1977).

Nanay, Bence. *Aesthetics as Philosophy of Perception* (New York: Oxford University Press, 2016).

Nash, Stephen. "The Empty Forests of Vietnam," *New York Times*, April 7, 2019, TR1.

Natta, Jr., Don Van, Adam Liptak, and Clifford J. Levy. "The Miller Case: A Notebook, a Cause, a Jail Cell and a Deal," *New York Times*, October 16, 2005, sec. 1, p. 1.

Nelson, Craig. *Thomas Paine: Enlightenment, Revolution, and the Birth of Modern Nations* (New York: Penguin, 2007).

Nexon, Daniel H., and Thomas Wright. "What's at Stake in the American Empire Debate," *American Political Science Review* 101, no. 2 (2007): 253–71.

Norton, Anne. *Leo Strauss and the Politics of American Empire* (New Haven: Yale University Press, 2004).

Oakes, James. *Freedom National: The Destruction of Slavery in the United States* (New York: W.W. Norton & Company, 2012).

Oreskes, Naomi, and Erik M. Conway. *The Collapse of Western Civilization: A View from the Future* (New York: Columbia University Press, 2014).

Osborn, Ronald E. *Humanism and the Death of God: Searching for the Good after Darwin, Marx, and Nietzsche* (New York: Oxford University Press, 2017).

Outram, Dorinda. *The Enlightenment*, 3rd ed. (New York: Cambridge University Press, 2013).

Oxtoby, Willard G., Roy C. Amore, and Amir Hussain. *World Religions: Eastern Traditions* 4th ed. (New York: Oxford University Press, 2014).

Padgett, Deborah K., Benjamin F. Henwood, and Sam J. Tsemberis. *Housing First: Ending Homelessness, Transforming Systems, and Changing Lives* (New York: Oxford University Press, 2015).

Palmer, Bryan D. *James P. Cannon and the Origins of the American Revolutionary Left, 1890–1928* (Urbana: University of Illinois Press, 2010).

Paolucci, Henry. "Introduction" in *Hegel: On the Arts*, Henry Paolucci, ed., 2nd ed. (Smyrna, DE: Griffon House, 2001).
Parr, Adrian. *The Wrath of Capital: Neoliberalism and Climate Change Politics* (New York: Columbia University Press, 2013).
Pear, Robert. "Trump Administration's Plea to Health Care Industry Surprises Experts," *New York Times*, November 25, 2018, A20.
———. "Eager to Sink Medicare Plan, Lobbies Unite," *New York Times*, February 24, 2019, A1.
Perkins, Robert L., ed. *History and System: Hegel's Philosophy of History* (Albany: State University of New York, 1984).
Pierre-Louis, Kendra. "U.S. Climate Study Has Grim Warning of Economic Risks," *New York Times*, November 24, 2018, A1.
———. "Emissions Surge, Hastening Perils across the Globe," *New York Times*, December 6, 2018, A1.
Piketty, Thomas. *Capital in the Twenty-First Century*, trans. Arthur Goldhammer (Cambridge, MA: Belknap Press, 2014).
Pillow, Kirk. *Sublime Understanding: Aesthetic Reflection in Kant and Hegel* (Cambridge, MA: MIT Press, 2000).
Plumer, Brad. "Wildlife Facing Extinction Risk All Over Globe," *New York Times*, May 7, 2019, A1.
Plumer, Brad, and Lisa Friedman. "Trump Has Allies on Fossil Fuels," *New York Times*, December 11, 2018, A1.
Polk, Sam. "For the Love of Money," *New York Times*, January 19, 2014, SR1.
Porter, Eduardo. "Technology Splits Work Force: High Pay for a Few and Low Pay for the Rest," *New York Times*, February 5, 2019, A17.
Porter, Jennifer E., and Darcess L. McLaren, eds. Star Trek *and Sacred Ground: Explorations of* Star Trek, *Religion, and American Culture* (Albany: State University of New York Press, 1999).
Rancière, Jacques. *Aesthetics and Its Discontents*, trans. Steve Corcoran (Malden, MA: Polity, 2009).
Rattansi, Ali. *Racism: A Very Short Introduction* (New York: Oxford University Press, 2007).
Rawls, John. *A Theory of Justice* (Cambridge, MA: Belknap, 1971).
Read, Christopher. *Lenin: A Revolutionary Life* (New York: Routledge, 2005).
Ricks, Thomas E. *Fiasco: The American Military Adventure in Iraq, 2003 to 2005* (New York: Penguin, 2007).
Rinehard, Christine Sixta. *Drones and Targeted Killing in the Middle East and Africa: An Appraisal of American Counterterrorism Policies* (Lanham, MD: Rowman & Littlefield, 2016).
Roberts, Robin. *Sexual Generations:* "Star Trek: The Next Generation" *and Gender* (Chicago: University of Illinois Press, 1999).
Robinson, William I. *A Theory of Global Capitalism: Production, Class, and State in a Transnational World* (Baltimore: Johns Hopkins University Press, 2004).
———. *Latin America and Global Capitalism: A Critical Globalization Perspective* (Baltimore: Johns Hopkins University Press, 2010).
Rockmore, Tom. *Marx's Dream: From Capitalism to Communism* (Chicago: University of Chicago Press, 2018).
Rogers, Katie. "Books Trump Can Praise without Reading a Word," *New York Times*, December 1, 2018, A18.
Roose, Kevin. "The Automation Agenda Hidden by the Davos Elite," *New York Times*, January 26, 2019, B1.
Rorty, Richard. *Philosophy and the Mirror of Nature* (Princeton: Princeton University Press, 1981).
Rosenberg, Alex. *How History Gets Things Wrong* (Cambridge, MA: MIT Press, 2018).
Rosenberg, Carol. "In Guantánamo Trials, Wrestling with Airing Evidence on Torture," *New York Times*, April 6, 2019, A1.

Rowe, C. Kavin. *One True Life: The Stoics and Early Christians as Rival Traditions* (New Haven: Yale University Press, 2016).

Ryan, Frank X., Brian E. Butler, and James A. Good, eds. *The Real Metaphysical Club* (Albany: State University of New York Press, 2019).

Sanger, David E., and William J. Broad. "U.S. Plans to End Nuclear Accord Signed by Russia," *New York Times*, February 2, 2019, A1.

Santora, Marc. "Poles Fear for Ancient Woodlands Despite Court Action," *New York Times*, April 10, 2019, A8.

Satariano, Adam, Raymond Zhong, and Daisuke Wakabayashi. "Putting the Squeeze on Huawei," *New York Times*, May 21, 2019, B1.

Savage, Charlie. "Order Limits Report of Deaths from U.S. Airstrikes," *New York Times*, March 7, 2019, A14.

Savage, Charlie. "Assange Indicted Over Leak as U.S. Expands Charges," *New York Times*, May 24, 2019, A1.

Savage, Charlie, and Maggie Haberman. "An Advocate of Presidential Power Interests Trump for Attorney General," *New York Times*, December 7, 2018, A15.

Schecter, Darrow. *The Critique of Instrumental Reason from Weber to Habermas* (New York: Bloomsbury Academic, 2012).

Schiff, Adam B. "Let the Military Run Drone Warfare," *New York Times*, March 13, 2014, A27.

Schmeink, Lars. *Biopunk Dystopias Genetic Engineering, Society and Science Fiction* (Liverpool: Liverpool University Press, 2017).

Schmitt, Carl. *The Concept of the Political*, expanded edition (Chicago: University of Chicago University, 2007 [1929]).

Schuessler, Jennifer. "With Canine Sex and Hooters, Pranks Jab at Academic Papers," *New York Times*, October 5, 2018, A1.

Schwalbe, Michael L. *Psychosocial Consequences of Natural and Alienated Labor* (Albany: State University of New York Press, 1986).

Schwartz, John. "400," *New York Times*, October 4, 2016, D3.

———. "'Like a Terror Movie': How Changing Climate Will Multiply Disasters," *New York Times*, November 20, 2018, A11.

———. "Will We Survive Climate Change?," *New York Times*, November 20, 2018, D7.

———. "In NOAA's Forecast, Flooding 'Worse Than Anything We've Seen in Recent Years,'" *New York Times*, March 22, 2019, A18.

Schwartz, Stephen P. *A Brief History of Analytic Philosophy: From Russell to Rawls* (West Sussex, UK: Wiley-Blackwell, 2012).

Sebell, Dustin. *The Socratic Turn: Knowledge of Good and Evil in an Age of Science* (Philadelphia: University of Pennsylvania Press, 2016).

Seefedt, Kristin S., and John D. Graham. *America's Poor and the Great Recession* (Bloomington: Indiana University Press, 2013).

Sellars, John. *Stoicism* (Los Angeles: University of California Press, 2006).

Selod, Saher. *Forever Suspect: Racialized Surveillance of Muslim Americans in the War on Terror* (Newark: Rutgers University Press, 2018).

Sengupta, Somini. "Coal Endangers a Planet Unable to Stop Using It," *New York Times*, November 25, 2018, A1.

Shane, Scott. "Waterboarding Used 266 Times on 2 Suspects," *New York Times*, April 20, 2009, A1.

Shanker, Thom. "Simple, Low-Cost Drones a Boost for U.S. Military," *New York Times*, January 25, 2013, A12.

Shear, Michael D. "Trump Imposes New Travel Ban on 7 Countries," *New York Times*, September 25, 2017, A1.

Shear, Michael D., and Maggie Haberman. "Trump Again Says Two Sides at Fault in Rally Violence," *New York Times*, August 16, 2017, A1.

Sides, John, Michael Tesler, and Lynn Vavreck. *Identity Crisis: The 2016 Presidential Campaign and the Battle for the Meaning of America* (Princeton: Princeton University Press, 2018).

Sinclair, Timothy J. *The New Masters of Capital: American Bond Rating Agencies and the Politics of Creditworthiness* (Ithaca: Cornell University Press, 2014).

Sklair, Leslie. *The Transnational Capitalist Class* (Malden, MA: Blackwell, 2001).

———. *Globalization: Capitalism and Its Alternatives* (New York: Oxford University Press, 2002).

Slater, Philip E. *Wealth Addiction* (New York: Dutton, 1980).

Slobodian, Quinn. *Globalists: The End of Empire and the Birth of Neoliberalism* (Cambridge, MA: Harvard University Press, 2018).

Smith, Mitch, and John Schwartz. "It's Bad, It's Real, Just Don't Call It Climate Change," *New York Times*, May 16, 20219, A10.

Smith, Steven B. "Leo Strauss: The Outlines of a Life," in *Cambridge Companion to Leo Strauss*, ed. Steven B. Smith (New York: Cambridge University Press, 2009).

Solnit, Rebecca. "Bird by Bird," *New York Times Magazine*, December 7, 2014, MM13.

Stack, Liam. "Manning Freed From Jail, But She May Return Soon," *New York Times*, May 10, 2019, A14.

Stevens, Matt, Megan Specia, and Patrick Kingsley. "Clinton Warns Europe of Peril of Open Doors," *New York Times*, November 23, 2018, A1.

Stevenson, Alexandra. "Xi Rallies His People As Trade War Intensifies," *New York Times*, May 22, 2019, A7.

Stiglitz, Joseph E. *Globalization and Its Discontents Revisited: Anti-Globalization in the Era of Trump* (New York: W.W. Norton, 2017).

Stock, Adam. *Modern Dystopian Fiction and Political Thought* (New York: Routledge, 2019).

Stolberg, Sheryl Gay. "Senate Rejects Bipartisan Challenge to Post-9/11 Presidential War Powers," *New York Times*, September 14, 2017, A15.

Stolberg, Sheryl Gay, and Brian M. Rosenthal. "White Nationalist Protest Leads to Deadly Violence," *New York Times*, August 13, 2017, A1.

Strange, Susan. *The Retreat of the State: The Diffusion of Power in the World Economy* (New York: Cambridge University Press, 1996).

Strauss, Leo. "Notes on Carl Schmitt, *The Concept of the Political*," in *The Concept of the Political*, expanded edition, by Carl Schmitt (Chicago: University of Chicago Press, 2007 [1932]).

Streitfeld, David. "A Ruse or Brilliant Marketing by Amazon? Yes," *New York Times*, November 7, 2018, B4.

Sugrue, Thomas J. *The Origins of the Urban Crisis: Race and Inequality in Postwar Detroit* (Princeton, NJ: Princeton University Press, 2005).

Suskind, Ron. "Faith, Certainty and the Presidency of George W. Bush," *New York Times Magazine*, October 17, 2004. Web.

Swanson, Ana, and Jim Tankersley. "As Trump Moves to End Trade War with China, Business Asks: Was It Worth It?," *New York Times*, March 5, 2019, B1.

Tabuchi, Hiroko. "The Banks Putting Rain Forests in Peril," *New York Times*, December 4, 2016, BU1.

———. "The Oil Industry's Covert Campaign to Rewrite American Car Emissions Rules," *New York Times*, December 13, 2018. Web.

Tanguay, Daniel. *Leo Strauss: An Intellectual Biography* (New Haven: Yale University Press, 2007).

Tavernise, Sabrina. "A New Country for Conflict Resolution Experts: The U.S.," *New York Times*, February 5, 2019, A12.

———. "Where Jobs Vanished, 'Nobody Had Our Backs,'" *New York Times*, May 28, 2019, A1.

Teachout, Zephyr. *Corruption in America: From Benjamin Franklin's Snuff Box to Citizens United* (Cambridge, MA: Harvard University Press, 2014).

"Ten States Still Have Fewer Jobs Since Recession," Reuters, March 25, 2016.

Thorsteinsson, Runar. *Roman Christianity and Roman Stoicism: A Comparative Study of Ancient Morality* (New York: Oxford University Press, 2013).

Tomasky, Michael. "America's Coming Oligarchy," *New York Times*, April 15, 2019, A23.

Tonelson, Alan. *The Race to the Bottom: Why a Worldwide Worker Surplus and Uncontrolled Free Trade are Sinking American Living Standards* (Boulder, CO: Westview, 2000).

"Transcript: Donald Trump's Taped Comments about Women," *New York Times*, October 8, 2016. Web.

Trapp, Michael, ed. *Socrates from Antiquity to the Enlightenment* (New York: Routledge, 2007).

Tuck, Richard. *Hobbes: A Very Short Introduction* (New York: Oxford University Press, 2002).

Turkewitz, Julie, and Coral Davenport. "Leader of Interior Dept. Resigns under Cloud of Ethics Inquiries," *New York Times*, December 16, 2018, A1.

Uchitelle, Louis. "Goodbye, Production (and Maybe Innovation)," *New York Times*, December 24, 2006, sec. 3 p. 4.

Van der Pijl, Kees. *Transnational Classes and International Relations* (New York: Routledge, 1998).

Varon, Elizabeth R. *Disunion!: The Coming of the American Civil War, 1789–1859* (Chapel Hill: University of North Carolina Press, 2010).

Vegso, Roland. *The Naked Communist: Cold War Modernism and the Politics of Popular Culture* (New York: Fordham University Press, 2013).

Verene, Donald Phillip. *Hegel's Absolute: An Introduction to Reading the Phenomenology of Spirit* (Albany: State University New York Press, 2007).

Vineyard, Jennifer. "Spoiler: The Villains in 'Our Planet' Are Humans," *New York Times*, April 9, 2019, C2.

Wachter, Susan M., and Kimberly A. Zeuli, eds. *Revitalizing American Cities* (Philadelphia: University of Pennsylvania Press, 2013).

Wagner, Jon, and Jan Lundeen. *Deep Space and Sacred Time:* Star Trek *in the American Mythos* (Westport, CT: Praeger, 1998).

Wakabayashi, Daisuke, and Alan Rappeport. "Arrest of a Top Huawei Executive Further Strains U.S.-China Ties," *New York Times*, December 6, 2018, A1.

Walsh, Declan, and Ihsanullan Tipu Mehsud. "Civilian Deaths in Drone Strikes Cited in Report," *New York Times*, October 22, 2013, A1.

Ward, Colin. *Anarchism: A Very Short Introduction* (New York: Oxford University Press, 2004).

Wedgwood, Ralph. *The Value of Rationality* (New York: Oxford University Press, 2017).

Westerhoff, Jan. *Reality: A Very Short Introduction* (New York: Oxford University Press, 2012).

Whippman, Ruth. "We're All in Sales Now," *New York Times*, November 25, 2018, SR1.

Wigelsworth, Jeffrey R. *Deism in Enlightment England: Theology, Politics, and Newtonian Public Science* (Manchester: Manchester University Press, 2009).

Williams, Timothy."For Shrinking Cities, Destruction Is a Path to Renewal," *New York Times*, November 12, 2013, A15.

Willse, Craig. *The Value of Homelessness: Managing Surplus Life in the United States* (Minneapolis: University of Minnesota Press, 2015).

Wingfield, Nick, and Patricia Cohen. "Let the Bidding Begin," *New York Times*, September 8, 2017, B1.

Winters, Jeffrey A. *Oligarchy* (New York: Cambridge University Press, 2011).

Winters, Jeffrey A., and Benjamin I. Page. "Oligarchy in the United States," *Perspectives on Politics* 7, no. 4 (2009): 731–51.

Wong, Edward, and Alan Rappeport. "U.S. and China Push Nations to Pick a Side," *New York Times*, November 22, 2018, A1.

Wu, Tim. *The Curse of Bigness: Antitrust in the New Gilded Age* (New York: Columbia Global Reports, 2018).

Yuan, Li. "Retooling China, from the Bottom Up," *New York Times*, July 5, 2018, B1.

———. "Some in China Fear Severing Ties with U.S.," *New York Times*, May 15, 2019, A1.

Zimmer, Carl. "Earth's Near-Death Experience," *New York Times*, December 11, 2018, D3.

———. "The Lost History of Biosphere 2," *New York Times*, March 31, 2019, SR1.

Zuquete, Jose Pedro. *The Identitarians: The Movement Against Globalism and Islam in Europe* (South Bend, IN: University of Notre Dame Press, 2018).

Index

About the Author

George A. Gonzalez (PhD, University of Southern California, 1997) is Professor of Political Science at the University of Miami. He has been at the University of Miami since 1999. Prof. Gonzalez's area of research specialization is U.S. environmental politics and policy (e.g., energy, pollution, global warming). His books include: *Energy and Empire: The Politics of Nuclear and Solar Power in the United States* (2012); *Energy and the Politics of the North Atlantic* (2013); *American Empire and the Canadian Oil Sands* (2016); as well as *Energy, the Modern State, and the American World System* (2018). Prof. Gonzalez has published research articles in *Polity* (the journal of the Northeastern Political Science Association). He has also published research articles in the journal of *Environmental Politics*, and in *Capitalism Nature Socialism*. In addition, Prof. Gonzalez has published original research in the journals of *Studies in American Political Development*, and *Public Integrity*.

Prof. Gonzalez also has a research agenda in the field of political theory and popular culture. In this area of study he has published articles in the journal *Foundation: The International Review of Science Fiction*, as well as the books *The Politics of Star Trek: Justice, War, and the Future* (2015); *The Absolute and Star Trek* (2017); *Star Trek and the Politics of Globalism* (2018); *Popular Culture as Art and Knowledge: A Critique of Authoritarian Neoliberalism and the Crisis of Democracy* (2019); and *Popular Culture and the Political Values of Neoliberalism* (2019). Through the vehicle of the broadcast iterations of the Star Trek franchise, Prof. Gonzalez comments on metaphysics, international relations, justice, pragmatism, ethics, and the American left.